MAKING BEAUTY WITH THE ASHES

How God Saved My Marriage

ELISHA MAGILL

Trilogy Christian Publishers
A Wholly Owned Subsidary of Trinity Broadcasting Network
2442 Michelle Drive
Tustin, CA 92780

For information, address Trilogy Christian Publishing
Rights Department, 2442 Michelle Drive, Tustin, Ca 92780.
Trilogy Christian Publishing/ TBN and colophon are trademarks of Trinity Broadcasting Network.

For information about special discounts for bulk purchases, please contact Trilogy Christian Publishing.

Manufactured in the United States of America

Trilogy Disclaimer: The views and content expressed in this book are those of the author and may not necessarily reflect the views and doctrine of Trilogy Christian Publishing or the Trinity Broadcasting Network.

10 9 8 7 6 5 4 3 2 1

Library of Congress Cataloging-in-Publication Data is available.

ISBN 978-1-64088-549-3 (Print Book)
ISBN 978-1-64088-550-9 (ebook)

CONTENTS

PREFACE

The definition of Redemption is: the act of saving or being saved from sin, error or evil. With that being said, I would like to take you on a journey with me. It is a journey full of happiness, sadness, betrayal, hurt, pain and ultimately... Redemption. I would like to take you on this journey with me right now and my prayer is that you will receive something from this book. That you will hear my heart, see what I have gone through in my life and what the Lord has redeemed me from.

I am not a professional writer, and some would call me the least qualified to write a book. Yet, here I am. I do not claim to know everything about life, but what I do know I will gladly share with you. I do not have all the answers, but I will do my best to point you in the direction of the One who does.

When Your World is Turned Upside Down!

The journey begins with a young woman who gets married to the man of her dreams. Anyone looking at them would believe they had a "perfect marriage". They started having babies and ended up having three children: two boys and one beautiful girl. Life was bliss, or so it appeared.

However, one day the husband decided to stray outside the home and enter an adulterous relationship. This was very painful for the woman. Yet, she decided to remain in the marriage and take her husband back; after all, he promised to never do it again. The husband strayed again and again and again. Each time he left his wife and three children abandoned and alone.

The fourth time the husband walked out on his family, the wife decided to end their marriage. Then, something happened! What happened, you might be asking? Well, let me share that with you by first telling you that I am the woman in the story.

I'm sure some of you are surprised and others probably already knew who I was talking about. My name is Elisha and it is my life experience that I am going to share with you. I have probably felt almost every emotion you can think of. I have known every feeling from extreme happiness to extreme pain. I've been high on the mountaintop and low in the valley. Through some of my worst moments, I hope to be able to share with you how the Lord, my God, helped me.

I was born in a Christian home with two very loving parents. They were a godly example to me, and I have many memories as a child seeing my parents serve the Lord. They took my two sisters and I to church every time the doors were opened. We attended all church functions and outings. You name it, my family was there.

My father was a deacon at the church we attended for many years. He served the church faithfully and had to walk through many tough decisions, but he maintained a standard of integrity through it all.

After many years of being a deacon, he and my mother decided to become the youth pastors at that same church. They held this position at the church for quite a number of years and were very faithful to it. The youth group flourished, with a large number attending every week. In fact, a lot of my fondest memories came from being so involved in the youth group.

I certainly had a lot of good role models around me during that time. I had a wonderful family at home, and a wonderful church family. I had what some would call a terrific life. And I did, I truly did.

Eventually, my dad received his calling from the Lord to pastor a church. He answered the call and followed God's leading. He started a small church that met in the "meeting room" of a hotel. They did this for many months until they started leasing a house and everyone met there.

From there he moved to a church building, and through the years has occupied several church buildings based on the fluctuations of attendance. He is still a pastor today.

I said all this, so you would have an idea of my upbringing. It was very exceptional. I am aware this is unusual and that a lot of children are not this fortunate, but I believe the Lord placed me in this home, with these two amazing parents for a specific reason.

Growing up with my parents, I witnessed their loving nature to each other. My father constantly sent my mother flowers. She owned her own flower shop, so he had to order them from one of her competitors.

My father was also very affectionate with my two sisters and me. He was always leaving us little love notes, sending us bags of candy to school or just going that extra mile to show us how much he cared. He really went over and above to show my sisters and I how loved we were. That is something I will never forget about my father. I will eternally be thankful for his unconditional love and support toward my sisters and me. He has shaped me into the woman I am today.

When I first met my husband, I was seventeen years old and a senior in high school. He was eighteen and a senior. We went to different schools, so our meeting was a rather interesting story. One evening, my sisters and I were grocery shopping with my mother at a local grocery store.

We were doing our usual browsing when we spied this young handsome man in an aisle we were passing by. We all thought he was very cute. I thought that would be the last encounter with the cute grocery boy.

A few weeks later, I was looking at a friend's yearbook. He just so happened to attend the same high school as the unnamed cute grocery boy. When I saw his picture, I was quite excited because I had never expected to see him beyond the grocery store.

I gave my friend one of my senior pictures and told him to show it to the cute grocery boy, who I now knew was named Brian. My friend did show Brian my picture and he thought I was cute too and even wanted me to call him.

Well, I was a very shy girl, and calling a boy was out of the question. So, he ended up having to call me. We fell head over heels for each other very fast. Within the first couple of months we were even talking marriage. Even though we were both still seniors in high school, something inside both of us knew, "this is the one."

We only dated for about six months when he "popped the question." I was completely surprised. We had been talking about marriage; yet, I did not expect him to propose when he did.

It happened at my high school graduation party my parents had given for me at our home. All my close friends and family were there. For some reason everyone knew he was going to propose except for me. He had already spoken to my father in advance and had received permission to ask me to marry him. Of course, I was told all of this after the fact.

During the party, Brian asked me to go the park with him. I was still completely clueless at this point. We went, and he took me to some picnic tables where we sat down and talked for a few minutes. I was still clueless! Then Brian stood up and got down on one knee. Still completely in the dark, I thought he was inviting me to sit down on his knee. He told me to stand and I kept trying to sit down!

This happened a couple times until he pulled out the ring. When I saw the ring, I knew what was going on then.

The tears began to flow at that point, and they continued to flow! I, of course, said yes. We embraced for a long time, and then headed back to my graduation party to share the news. I was ecstatic! I knew that our marriage was going to be just like my parents' marriage. Perfect!

We spent ten months preparing for our big day. Everything just flowed so effortlessly. My mother owned a flower shop, so she was able to do all the flowers for a low price. I found my wedding dress very quickly. Everything was so smooth and stress free. It was like we were meant to be.

We were so in love and all we wanted to do was get married and spend the rest of our lives together. We even attended marriage counseling a couple months before we were married with my aunt and uncle, who were also pastors. We were ready!

On April 12, 1997, at 7:00 p.m., Brian Magill and Elisha McCullum became husband and wife. It was a beautiful, scripturally based ceremony. God was the center of the entire engagement. Things were going to be great. Our happily ever after had finally begun.

Our honeymoon was in Panama City, FL. We enjoyed spending every minute with each other; however, we left a couple days early because we both ended up getting sun poisoning and were miserable with itching. That didn't spoil anything though, because we were so in love and every moment together was worth it, even if it involved itching like crazy.

Our first home was an apartment, which was over the top of my parent's garage. My father had turned it into an apartment for us to start off our lives together. We were both very thankful, and Brian helped him with the construction part of it.

It was so fun watching my father and husband work together. I just knew Brian was going to turn out exactly like my dad. We spent the first three years of our marriage right there in that little one bedroom, one bath apartment.

Our first year of marriage was wonderful. We loved spending time with each other and we found jobs to help support our growing marriage. Everything we did, we did together. We were learning more and more about each other. How could anything go wrong? This was how it was going to be forever!

To our surprise, after our first year of wedded bliss, our marriage started getting rocky. We were trying to learn to adjust to one another, but we were still teenagers ourselves. When conflict arose, we didn't know how to handle it maturely, so yelling at each other started to develop. It seemed like the right thing to do; after all, we were both angry.

I came from a home where my parents displayed love and affection on a regular basis. That was my normal and that was what I expected. My expectations were very high. Brian also came from a loving home, but the love and affection shown was not what I was used to.

My parents rarely fought, so I was quite taken back when Brian and I did. I didn't know about taking responsibility for words and actions. I would just say whatever I wanted when I was angry, and he did the same.

I expected to have a marriage exactly like my parents and set the bar pretty high for Brian. In fact, he would have had to be an Olympic high jumper to cross this bar I set. I think subconsciously I was looking for him to treat me the way my father did. And Brian needed to do it without me asking. He should've just known, but he didn't. My expectations were impossible for anyone to meet.

Since we lived in my parent's garage turned into an apartment, they began to witness the yelling and fighting. They tried to help us and counseled with us quite a bit. It did help some, but we were both very young and just wanted the other person to change. We had the mindset, "if someone needed to change, it was going to be you."

I had a job working at the hospital in the ER registration department and Brian was a press operator for a press company. We decided we needed to find a new home and wanted to build. We found a piece of land we both loved so we got a loan and the building process began.

It took almost a year to build our dream home, which was a cape cod style and we both were in love with it. My grandfather was a retired builder and helped my husband out quite a bit. Brian really learned how to build very quickly. It was almost as if he was born to do this. My grandfather was even amazed at how quickly he grasped the understanding of how to build a house. Our home was beautiful, and we were ready to start a new chapter of our lives.

Brian and I had been talking about having a baby shortly after we moved into our dream home. It was a big step for us. We had only been married for about three years at this point, but we both wanted kids, so we decided to go ahead and give it a try. I had been off birth control for about one year; still, there was no pregnancy.

I started to get very concerned. I was in and out of the doctor's office several times with no answer as to why this was happening. Finally, at one of my appointments, they tried a different test and discovered I had a pituitary tumor. This news scared me to death!

I had all these thoughts running through my mind when I heard the word "tumor". I had relatives pass away from cancerous tumors, as I'm sure many of you reading this can relate. Tumor is never a word you want to hear.

An MRI was ordered to see the size of the tumor and to find out if it was malignant or benign. Just the word tumor alone scared me to death. Thankfully, the results came back that the tumor was benign; however, I would need to go on medication to shrink the size of the tumor. Therefore, we decided to put having a baby on hold for a while because of the health scare I had.

A few months later, Brian and I discussed the possibility of me enrolling into nursing school. It was something I had really wanted to do for a long time. After talking about it, we decided to put having a baby on hold for even longer.

About four years into our marriage, I started nursing school. I went to school during the day and Brian worked a second shift job. We didn't see each other very much during that year. We didn't have cell phones at that time either because they were a new technology and very expensive. The only way I could communicate with him during the day was on a payphone in the cafeteria of the school. It was a very difficult year for our marriage.

About half way into nursing school I unexpectedly became pregnant. The news shocked us both, but we were equally excited. At the beginning of the pregnancy, I had a considerable amount of morning sickness. It was very difficult going to clinicals in the hospital during my first trimester, but fortunately I had some good nursing school friends who helped me out in those situations where I could not handle smells and bodily fluids.

I was able to graduate nursing school in December 2001 without any complications due to my pregnancy. After graduation, I ended up getting a job at a local University Hospital. It all happened right before Christmas and it looked like the next year was going to be a pretty great year. Everything seemed perfect...and then heartache struck!

2

To Be or Not to Be

I had just finished nursing school and was a couple of months away from delivering our first child. At that time, our marriage was extremely rocky. We didn't see each other very much and we argued a lot more than we didn't.

There was a definite "disconnect" in our marriage and neither of us really wanted to address it. Instead, blaming the other person always seemed to work best. And that is when Brian decided to walk out the door on our marriage, when I was 8 months pregnant. I was devastated! I didn't know what to do.

I was pregnant with our first baby and very afraid. Even though both of us had threatened to walk out the door many times before, I didn't mean those words and I assumed he didn't either. But he did, and my world was turning upside down.

My parents asked me to come stay with them because they didn't want me living alone being so big and pregnant.

So, I moved out of the house Brian and I had built together, and Brian moved back in. Here I was, facing the world as a potential single mom to our first child. I was very afraid to say the least.

At this time I was on maternity leave shortly after starting my first job as a nurse. I would get up every morning with my parents and go to the church with them. Most of the time I felt like a burden. They were trying to help me pass the time and not dwell on what was going on in my life and my mind.

My mom would take me to the mall and walk with me to try to induce labor even though I didn't know if I was ready to have the baby yet. I was going to be a single mom and a first-time mom all in one. The thought of that was too much to bear. I cried myself to sleep more times than not.

My parents were very supportive and helped me in any way they could. My father would bring the "baby" home a hot fudge cake because he knew the "baby" would need one. He was a lifesaver to me during that time.

I would sit up late and talk with him; well, I would mostly cry with him. A lot of times he would try to help advise me, but most of the time he would just listen while I cried. He is everything a Dad should be. He held me together when I felt like I was falling apart. My mom did too, but there is something about a girl's relationship with her father.

I went through baby showers just trying not to fall apart. Everyone knew my situation and I felt like all eyes were on me, watching to see if I really would fall to pieces. I would open gift after gift and wonder, how am I going to do this? How am I going to care for a baby when I don't even know what I'm doing? Each gift seemed to cut a little deeper. The pain was indescribable.

Then on February 5th around 10 p.m., I started having contractions. After waiting a while and recording all the contraction times, my mom decided it was time to head to the hospital. She called Brian and told him I was in labor. He was at work at the time, so he took off and headed to the hospital to meet me. This was not the ideal way I wanted to experience the birth of my first child.

When I got to the hospital, they took me to labor and delivery right away for a labor check. My pregnancy was 38 weeks at this point. I had not dilated very much, but my doctor decided to keep me and began to induce labor. I was in labor all through the night. My mom and sisters were all there with me in the delivery room, but Brian's presence in the room caused tensions to soar. Everyone was very upset with him and that is putting it lightly.

Our first child, Hunter Blake Magill, made his appearance on Feb. 6, 2002, at 8:02 a.m. The doctor made it to the hospital just in time to catch him as he entered the world. He was a very small baby boy. He only weighed 5 lbs. 15 oz and was 19 inches long.

I was so very nervous to hold him and feed him or do anything with him for that matter. He was just so tiny to me. Brian stayed in the hospital with me that first day then ended up leaving during the night.

When he left, 1 felt very alone. Here I was…in a hospital room and with a new baby for the first time in my life. It was a very traumatic experience for me. I never thought that the birth of my first child would be like this. I always imagined it to be a joyous occasion, not one filled with fear, tears, and pain.

I tried to cling to God during this time of my life. I prayed and sought Him as much as I could. I needed Him more than ever in my life. In those moments when I thought

I was going to fall apart, I would call out to the Lord and immediately I'd feel His peace calm me. I had to cry out to Him a lot during this time.

When I was released from the hospital, Brian was there to get me; however, he drove me back to my parent's house and dropped me off. Once again, this was not how I pictured the birth of my first baby. I felt like a burden to practically everyone. And I felt abandoned and rejected by the love of my life.

About a week after leaving the hospital and staying with my parents, there was a knock at their door. When I went to answer it, I was startled to see the sheriff standing there. Of course, when I answered the door I was holding my newborn in my arms. And when the sheriff saw that sweet little baby boy, he began to apologize for what he had to do.

He handed me divorce papers and instantly I began crying. I tried to hold back the tears but there was no stopping them. My emotions were raw at that point. I hated crying in front of the sheriff because I knew this was part of his job he did not like. I took the papers and slowly closed the door. What was I going to do now?

I literally felt like I was slowly dying inside. There was so much pain I didn't know what to do. How much more could I take? My world was caving in all around me. I cried out to God with everything inside of me. In fact, crying was pretty much what I did most of the time anyway.

I loved my new baby, but I was broken; therefore, caring for him took a lot from me. When you're broken, you really don't have much of yourself to give anyone. Everyone closes to me tried to help me as best as they knew how during this time.

My father reached out to a good Christian counselor and she began to help me cope with all of what I was going through. I was still praying and crying out to God for answers. Although I didn't get a response to why all of this was happening, He did give me peace in the storm.

Sometimes He doesn't calm the storm in our lives, but He takes time to hold us during the storm. That is exactly what He did for me. Even though the divorce storm was swirling around me, God held me in His peace so many times.

After many discussions, I talked Brian into letting me move back into our house. After all, most of the stuff I needed to care for the baby was there. He was not happy about it at first, but then decided I could move in. I did, and he moved out. My heart was crushed.

My parents stayed with me at night for about a week to help me adjust with taking care of a newborn baby. Having them at the house overnight helped tremendously. They are a true blessing from God.

It didn't appear as if life could get any worse for me at this point. Emotionally I was very dejected; thankfully, my parents were able to be the strong backbone I needed during this time. I really leaned on their strength as they encouraged me and helped me not to completely break down.

At this time, I really began to draw close to the Lord as well. I knew I could not survive constantly on my parent's strength, but neither could I do it on my own. I reached out to Him for help and I received a strength I didn't know I had.

The Lord began to really show me that He was present at many moments of my life. For instance, when I thought I was all by myself, He would show me exactly where He was the whole time. I was never alone. He was right there holding me, protecting me, and giving me the strength to make it through one more day.

I decided I was going to fight for our marriage. Even though Brian wanted out and had filed for divorce, I was not going to let the devil take away what God had placed together. I stood in faith and expected to see God move mightily on my behalf. Even though I didn't see it, I had faith that God would work things out.

When Hunter was born, he had a sacral dimple at the top of his bottom, just above the crease between the buttocks. They did an ultrasound at the hospital just to be sure the dimple was closed. If it was not closed, there could be exposure to the spine. Thank the Lord that was not our case!

About a month after Hunter was born, I noticed some bleeding from that dimple. I called my parents and we quickly rushed him to a pediatric hospital ER in our area. I called Brian on the way there and he met me at the hospital.

We were in the ER for many hours. They did x-rays and blood work. So many thoughts and fears for my baby ran through my mind. However, everything was fine. The dimple was still closed. The skin had become irritated and bled because some of his stool had gotten inside the dimple. That was such a huge relief!

We left the ER relieved that nothing was wrong with our baby. Brian ended up coming back to the house with me and stayed for the night. I must admit that it felt nice having my family all under the same roof, even though it took a trip to the ER to make it happen.

Brian stayed the next night, and the next, and before I knew it, he was living back in our house. We didn't even have a conversation about him moving back in, it just happened. To say the least, I was still very hurt and scared. He was home, but he was still not treating me well. As for me, I was angry and fearful.

We finally talked about things and decided we would see the marriage counselor I had been seeing while I was pregnant. And we would see the counselor together. She came over to our home since we had a newborn and had the marriage counseling sessions there.

I was so thankful for her. She helped us work through some of our issues. We decided to work things out and work toward our marriage. A month after we got back together, we celebrated our 5-year wedding anniversary. I was thankful to God that we were back together.

When Bad Meets Worse

Brian and I had been separated for a couple months until he returned home wanting to reconcile. I thought things were going to be ok after that. I thought if I constantly showed him the error of his way, he would never walk out the door again. I believed that to keep him from repeating a behavior, I needed to remind him of what he had done. And I did it all the time. Well…that doesn't work.

In March of 2007, I found out I was pregnant. It was a surprise pregnancy but nonetheless we were very excited. Hunter was 2 years old by this time and the thought of adding another brother or sister was very exciting! Brian and I had been back together for a couple years, things were looking up and this new pregnancy was the icing on the cake.

I scheduled my first OB appointment with glee. They did all the regular things they do for your first appointment and I loved it all. My mother worked at this OB office, so they took me back for an ultrasound to get a peek at my little bundle of joy. The Ultrasound Tech placed the probe on my stomach, but because I was too early they had to do an internal ultrasound.

The Ultrasound Tech found the yolk sac where the baby is, but there was no heartbeat detected. She tried and tried but could not detect a heartbeat. Tears instantly began to flow.

It was then that I realized I had lost the baby. My mother led me out the side door of the office and drove me home because I was crying so hard. I called Brian on the way home to tell him the devastating news. My heart was crushed.

The office set up a D&C, which is a Dilation and Curettage. It's a procedure to remove tissue from inside the uterus, which is simply clearing the uterus after a miscarriage. On the day of the procedure, I was quite tearful as I prepared to leave the house. As Brian and I were walking out the door, the phone rang. I answered, and it was my doctor. She told me she had decided to postpone my D&C for another week.

Since we were unclear of the time I got pregnant, she said it's possible I would not be far enough along in my pregnancy to detect a heartbeat. Therefore, she wanted me to wait a week and then come back in for labs. By that time, it would be easier to see if I had indeed lost the baby.

I had a glimmer of hope! For the first time I started entertaining the thought that my baby may still be alive. It was a very hope filled week and yet very agonizing. I didn't want to get too excited because there was still the possibility that I had miscarried.

The very long week was finally over, and I headed into the office to have my blood work done. I was extremely nervous. The fate of my baby was on the line. I watched as the lab girl drew my blood. I kept praying and praying that the results would come back good and that my baby was going to be fine.

The next day Brian and I headed back into the office. We sat nervously in the room waiting for the doctor to come and deliver the news. She walked in, sat down, and pulled her paper from her folder. She looked me in the eyes and said, "Your numbers went down. I'm sorry but you are having a miscarriage." Those words felt as if they literally pierced my heart. All the hopes I had of seeing my baby or even holding my baby was gone. My heart broke!

Two weeks later I went into the hospital to have a D&C performed. I was devastated. Sure, the pregnancy was a surprise; however, from the moment I found out I was pregnant, my heart instantly loved that little one I had never met. It won't be until I get to heaven that I'll get to see my sweet baby. I cannot wait until I get there and see this little person run up to me and jump into my arms.

Thankfully Brian was by my side during this very difficult time and helped me in any way he could. Miscarriage is a silent pain that not many people talk about. I felt very alone even though Brian was right there beside me. It's a pain that is hard to talk about and share with others. I prayed a lot during this time. And I felt God was right beside me, giving me His peace. At times when I wanted to just crumble into a corner, I would feel his peace come over me.

After losing our baby, I realized that we were ready for more children and Brian agreed. About seven months later I became pregnant again. I was very scared to say the least. At our first OB visit, they did an ultrasound to see how far along I was. There was no heartbeat. I was devastated.

The doctor assured me they would do another one in a week because it may still be too early to tell. The same scenario seemed to be happening again. For a whole agonizing week, I had to wait to see if I had lost another baby.

By the time the week had rolled around, I was a nervous wreck. They did an internal ultrasound and I leaped for joy when I saw the fluttering on the screen. My baby had a heartbeat! I cried tears of joy this time. My baby was alive!

I was extremely delighted and contented during the whole pregnancy. And the pregnancy was an easy one. There was no morning sickness like there had been with my first one. I felt great.

At this time, I had a job at a hospital working the night shift. Since my pregnancy was easy, with no complications, I was able to work up until 36 weeks. Then, I had to stop working because a hernia was being aggravated due to the pregnancy.

Finally, I delivered a beautiful baby girl. We named her Halle Blayre Magill, and she weighed 7lbs 7oz and was 20 inches long. She had her daddy's nose and her mama's eyes and blonde curly hair. She was perfect and the most beautiful baby girl we could have ever asked for.

Right before I gave birth to Halle, we had put our house up for sale and it ended up selling very quickly, which took us completely by surprise. We weren't expecting it to sell that fast. In fact, we hadn't even started building our next house at that time.

As a result, we moved in with my parents while our new house was being built. My parents had a full house because at that time, my other sister and her children, along with her newborn, had moved in with my parents while their house was being built also. Although it was a full house, it was nice having my mom and sister around.

My husband was the builder of our home and he did a wonderful job. It was the most beautiful home we had yet.

We eventually moved in when Halle was about two months old and Hunter had just turned four years old. Life was good. We had a big beautiful home, lived in a nice neighborhood, and lived close to my parents.

I went back to work at the hospital, and Brian continued building houses. The kids were healthy and growing. Our marriage was doing wonderful. We were moving forward with the past issues we had. I was healing from the pain of our marital issues and a miscarriage. Of course, seeing my baby girl everyday definitely helped with that. Nothing could be better, or so I thought.

The Phone Call

One morning my happy world felt like it came crashing down around me. I was awakened around 6:30 in the morning to our phone ringing. Brian had already headed off to work. At this point, he was working for a Heating and A/C business with a friend of his because the construction business had slowed down.

I usually didn't answer the phone if it rang that early, but something inside me told me to answer it, so I did. On the other end of the line was a man asking for Brian. I told him Brian was not there. I assumed it was the guy he was working for because Brian had just left the house.

Then the words that followed would forever change my life. The man said, "They are still together." I paused for a moment because I wasn't sure what he meant by that statement. He continued, "She told me it was over, but I found out they have still been seeing each other."

I had a rush of blood run to my face when I heard those words. I thought for sure this man had called and upset the wrong woman. The man was very angry and was quite mean with me on the phone. I kept asking him questions because I just couldn't believe what I was hearing.

At this point the man realized that everything he was telling me I was hearing for the first time. He thought I already knew that my husband was having an affair with his wife. And it had been going on for some time. I started crying on the phone. The man became apologetic that he was the one telling me about the affair.

I got off the phone and called Brian right away. I told him he needed to come home immediately, but I did not mention why. Then I called my parents and thankfully my mom had not left for work yet. She was getting ready to walk out the door but decided to get the phone. I was crying hysterically on the other end of the line. She and my dad came over to our house right away. They got there before Brian did, which was a good thing. I was very upset, and I don't know what I would've done had they not been there first.

Brian walked in the door to find my parents and I sitting in the living room. It was still early in the morning, so the children were asleep. Then the confrontation began. I asked him about the affair and he admitted to it. He told me that it had been going on for almost a year and that he had been trying to cut it off. He didn't because she kept threatening to tell me if he did.

I, of course, did not believe a word he spoke. He admitted it was a sexual relationship, which destroyed my already fragile heart. To think of your husband being intimate with another woman is something no one should ever have to think about. This was my reality now.

How could this happen? He swore to love only me. I didn't know what I was going to do. I told him he needed to break things off with the other woman. I made him go stay at his parent's house for a few nights because I needed time to think. Frankly, I didn't really want to look at him. I didn't know if I wanted to stay with him or if I even could stay with him. I had never experienced pain like that before in my life. It's a pain that can't be compared…it cuts very deep.

After a few days, I allowed him to come back home. He wanted to stay together but I didn't know what I wanted to do yet. I walked around in a state of shock for several weeks. I cried, but I still felt numb from the news. The reality of what had been done hadn't truly registered yet—the betrayal, the lies, and the unfaithfulness. How was I ever going to be able to trust him again? How was I ever going to be able to love him again? This was a betrayal of a bigger magnitude. Even in the Bible the Lord gives a way out for adultery.

Matthew 19:9 (NASB)—"And I say to you, whoever divorces his wife, except for immorality, and marries another woman commits adultery."

I read that scripture many times, trying to give myself a reason to leave him. I knew what the Bible said, but I also knew God was tugging at my heart to stay. It was very difficult, and I tried to give my pain to God as best I could. I was filled with so many emotions—anger, hurt, fear, and revenge. The unfaithfulness of a spouse is a very hard thing to deal with. It's a betrayal like none I have ever known. I struggled with self-worth, rejection, and eventually sank into a depression.

I needed help. There was a couple at my dad's church that had dealt with infidelity also. We met with them on several occasions and talked about what had happened. They shared with Brian and I what they had experienced and how God had healed their marriage. It gave me hope to see a couple on the other side of this unbearable pain I was now feeling. They helped us tremendously and even came out to our house on occasion to talk.

This same couple urged us to attend a marriage retreat for couples in desperate situations like ours. I was reluctant because I still didn't really know how I felt. I wanted to try to make things work; yet I was scared to at the same time.

After Brian and I talked about it, we decided to attend the retreat. I thought to myself, "If this retreat doesn't help, then I am done with the marriage." Honestly, I placed a high stake on the success of the retreat and on God.

It was an intensive three-day retreat in Cincinnati. We dug deep into our relationship over those days and it really helped me with my decision. And the decision was that I wanted to stay in our marriage and work on it.

It was very difficult, but I knew God would be with me during this painful time of my life. I knew He heard me when I prayed and when most of the time I just cried. I knew He was there. I could feel Him around me. He gave me strength again and helped me to find the strength I didn't know I had.

He sent strong women my way to minister to me or give me a word of encouragement. He was looking out for me, especially now when I needed it most. I had always told myself before, if my husband ever cheats on me… I'm gone!

Now I was facing the very words I had spoken, and I was, ironically, taking a different route. No one can judge your decision to stay or leave until they have walked in your shoes. Every decision is different and should be based on what the Lord tells you to do. That's why listening to the voice of God in desperate situations is so important.

Sometimes His voice would come as a still small voice within. Other times He would speak through a song or send a person to give me an encouraging word. God desires to communicate with us and help us in our lives.

We just need to make ourselves available to listen. I always find that when my life is falling apart, my ears are more in tune to the Lord. In the middle of my pain and desperation, seeking Him helps bring peace into the chaotic situation.

Returning home from the retreat, we both had a desire in our hearts that we were going to make it work no matter what. We sold our second house and moved into a home in a different town. We moved into a subdivision where the houses were very close together. We were not used to living that close to people.

The lots were very small, and everyone's backyard fences touched the neighbor's fence. The last neighborhood we lived in had two-acre lots, so we had plenty of room. However, we were struggling financially, so selling our home and moving to this smaller home with smaller acreage was what we needed to do.

I was still struggling with the pain of the affair and trusting him again. We decided that we would start going to marriage counseling to help us get through this. Brian was very willing to do whatever he could to help me heal. He went right along with me and did whatever I asked of him. I am thankful that the Lord led us to a Christian marriage counselor. She was a tremendous help.

While we were in marriage counseling, I found out I was pregnant with our third child. This time I was devastated. I was already going through so much pain from the affair, now here I was pregnant just a few short months later.

I knew that my body would be changing, and that I would be gaining weight. All the lies of the enemy started pouring in—"He didn't want you before, he definitely won't want you now. He will run out the door again and find someone else. He'll leave you alone during another pregnancy."

As you can imagine, my mind was filled with these tormenting thoughts. That first week I found out I was pregnant I cried more than I didn't. Then I started thinking, "Why wasn't I happy I was pregnant?" This thought made me cry more. It was a terribly emotional cycle I was on.

During this time, I went to a women's ministry meeting at our church. I decided I needed to be around women who loved the Lord and would pray. During that meeting, I received a prophetic word about the baby I was carrying.

The Lord had a plan for this bundle of surprise. In fact, this child was not a surprise, but planned by the Lord.

Sometimes things in our life can look like 'bad timing' but to God who sees the big picture, my baby was right on time.

I had just gotten a new job at a hospital down the road from where we lived. I had to let my bosses know I was pregnant. I was so nervous because I had just started the job. They were very understanding and tried to help me out. Fortunately, with this baby I had no morning sickness and felt good for the majority of the time. My emotions were up and down. The affair was forever fresh in my mind, which made it hard to cope. Our marriage counselor helped me in every way she could.

A couple of months later, on Valentine's Day, I went out to get the mail. I opened our satellite bill and to my surprise, I saw that some of the purchased movies were pornographic.

When Brian got home I confronted him about the movies. He admitted that he had been watching these movies and went on to apologize.

I didn't know what to do. All the devastation and hurt I was feeling fell on me like a ton of bricks. It was as if I was suffocating. I remember thinking, "Lord, I can't take anymore! I'm just one person and this one person is about to die!" Over and over these depressive feelings, the pain, and the deep hurt kept crashing over me. I started to associate the pornography with the affair, and the affair with the pornography. They both coupled together and became massive in my mind. I was angry and very hurt.

I was so angry that I put all his clothes into a box. I was done, and he was leaving. I felt destroyed. It was like he had cheated on me all over again. How can I heal when the scab is continuously being ripped off? I was very angry and disgusted. How could he do that to me?

All the promises he had made were now nothing in my mind. He told me he had been ordering porn and watching it when I went to work. By this time, I felt like I was not enough. How could I compare to all of this?

I could feel the anger and bitterness seeping in. At this point it had gotten harder to fight off these emotions because there was so much to be angry about. And here I was, pregnant with our third child. I didn't see how this could be part of God's plan. How could all of this be part of His plan? How could all this hurt be a part of His grand design? I questioned God quite regularly because I had a lot of things I just didn't understand. How could all this bad happen to my family and I?

We continued going to marriage counseling. At this point, it was starting to look like we may never get out of marriage counseling. I was an emotional mess with the pregnancy hormones and the fresh hurts that had been caused. I was having a difficult time coping.

We met with our counselor almost every week. Our situation was acute and volatile. Our marriage counselor stayed committed to us and helped in any way she could. Sometimes I think she was 'on call' just for us.

In September of that year, I gave birth to our surprise baby. We had decided to keep the baby's sex a surprise since that was how it started. Hayden Bryce Magill was born into the world weighing 6 lbs 1 oz and was 19 inches long.

I didn't know at the time, but our little surprise baby turned out to be the glue that held our family together during this devastating time. What the enemy tried to kill and destroy, God brought forth life from in the midst of it.

We still to this day call Hayden the glue to our family. This pregnancy was a surprise, but a bigger blessing that we needed and didn't know we needed. God can do anything during our pain. He hears every prayer and sees every tear. He holds our tears in the palm of His hand.

> **Psalms 56:8 (NASB)—You have taken account of my wanderings; Put my tears in Your bottle. Are they not in Your book?**

This scripture tells me that not only does God see every tear I cry, He collects them and remembers them. So, when you are in a painful situation, and do not think anyone knows or hears, remember that God sees every tear, collects them and remembers them. That is an awesome God we serve! This was something I experienced firsthand. There were a lot of nights I would just cry myself to sleep. God must have a lot of bottles full of my tears.

The Eye of The Storm

After having our third child, I went through a time of healing. We were still going to counseling about one day a week, sometimes two if I needed the extra help. We stuck with it and the Lord brought a lot of healing to my heart during this time.

Brian and I had a couple of good years healing together. I couldn't believe how well I was doing considering what we had gone through. I began to really think I could do this. I could be a help to women somewhere that had gone through the betrayal of adultery and come out on the other side. Then my third heartbreak occurred.

Brian and I started going through another rough patch. We were fighting a lot during that time. Then Brian decided he was going to walk out the door on me and our three children. I was shattered and that is putting it very, very lightly.

I was just starting to heal, and the scab was ripped right off again. Now, I felt like I was gushing blood from this gaping hole in my heart. I am one person. How can so much bad happen to one person? How could this happen again?

During this dark time of my life, I began questioning the Lord's love for me. Was He the one who allowed this to happen? If not, did He let it happen? Why didn't He stop this? My attention was turned to God, but not for help as before. Instead I became angry at Him.

I turned away from the Lord for a little bit. I was very angry, hurt, bitter, sad, overwhelmed and if I'm going to be honest, suicidal at times. I had my three children, which helped to keep me on this side of earth, but the pain was too excruciating.

I cried myself to sleep almost every night. The next morning my eyes were all swollen from the night before. It was a very dark time for me. I thought many times about walking away from God. Thankfully, my upbringing in church proved to be a stronger force than what the enemy had planned for my life.

> *1 Peter 5:8 (NASB)—Be of sober spirit, be on alert. Your adversary, the devil, prowls around like a roaring lion, seeking someone to devour.*

This scripture tells me that the enemy is always looking, always seeking for someone's life to kill, someone to destroy. I felt like he had cross hairs on my life during this time. Even during my time of anger, doubt and unbelief, God never left me alone. He sent people from our church to minister to me.

God was sending people my way left and right. He was not going to allow the enemy to have the final say in my life. The enemy was not going to write my final chapter. I know that now, but then all I could see was hurt and pain. God knew that, He knows us better than we know ourselves.

> *Romans 8:28 (NASB)—And we know that God causes all things to work together for good to those who love God, to those who are called according to His purpose.*

He knew me. He knows me. He knew I needed extra help during this time. He had people call me, reach out to me, and encourage me during this time. The Lord knows me; He knew this time was difficult for me and He made every effort to help me get through. I didn't see it at the time but looking back over all the sadness in my life, I can clearly see where God had His hand over me. He protected me from the enemy and what the enemy was trying to do to me and through me.

The enemy was constantly battling my mind, which is his battleground. I was always hearing day in and day out—"What did I do to deserve this?" The enemy was not only throwing pain and grief my way, but also helping me to become a victim.

And by this time, I was getting pretty good at it. "With what I had been through, who could blame me?" This was how I was thinking. "Who wouldn't be bitter and angry? I've been through more than what most women will go through their whole lifetime."

The enemy was having a field day with me and I was soaking it all in. After all, "this had been done to me without just cause. I was a faithful wife. I never walked out on my family. I didn't deserve this." The enemy was getting good at getting through to me. I was becoming more and more bitter by the day. And bitterness likes company.

Be careful who you have around you for comfort during difficult times. The enemy is very good about strategically placing people who will agree with everything you say. Before long, you feel better ripping people apart with your words. It becomes a fix. And instead of just a gathering, it becomes a homicide scene.

> *Psalms 1:1 (NASB)—How blessed is the man who does not walk in the counsel of the wicked, Nor stand in the path of sinners, Nor sit in the seat of scoffers!*

After nine months of separation I was still struggling every day to get out of bed and take care of my three children. And now Brian wanted to come back home. I did not agree to this at first. I was very angry.

Following several weeks of talking and many promises being made, I decided to concede and let him return home. I was very leery and did not trust him at all. I was basically waiting for him to leave again.

We got back into marriage counseling right away. I do believe we were becoming pros at marriage counseling by now. It was during our time of trying to reconcile that he revealed to me there had been two other women he had slept with during our time apart.

This only threw me into a whirlwind of anger. I even became combative at one point while we were driving to a counseling session. After all, I felt very entitled to display all anger I was feeling. I considered it my right to express my feelings and if that included smacking my husband in the truck, then I did just that.

Not only was the enemy trying to destroy my marriage and husband at this time, he was trying to destroy me as well. If he could keep me bound in anger, rage and bitterness, then he has got me good.

I was entangled in one deadly web; however, it was deadly only to me. What I was experiencing took me a long while to come out of. I felt like a victim so therefore I deserved to be angry. Being angry is not a sin; after all, I did have reason to be angry, but when anger consumes you to the point it had me, then it is a sin.

> *Ephesians 4:26–27 (NASB)—"BE ANGRY, AND YET DO NOT SIN; do not let the sun go down on your anger, and do not give the devil an opportunity.*

In other words, this verse is saying that if you go to bed angry, you will wake up angry and in doing so, open a door to the enemy to come in and wreak havoc in your life. I burned with anger.

I could feel it in my chest and my heart would race. Sometimes I didn't even feel alive until I would get angry. The anger had consumed me at this point. And that was the whole plan of the enemy. His plan was to destroy my husband, destroy my family and ultimately destroy me.

He will use things that other people have done to you to destroy you. Even if it was no fault of your own and you didn't bring these emotions on yourself, he will still use that to destroy you. The enemy does not play fair; he never has, and he never will.

Brian was home for about three months. I'm sure my anger was too much to bear and that is when my fourth heartbreak happened. He walked out the door of our marriage again. This door was steadily a revolving door, which I called our marriage.

By now I had no hope. Everything I believed could happen between us was gone. I finally threw in the towel. I had decided at this point there was nothing here worth salvaging. Everyone around me was on my side at this point.

My ears were filled on a daily basis with—"you deserve better", "he has done this one time too many", "he will never change", "it's time for you to move on with your life". I agreed. I tried to pray, stay close to God, but I still looked at Him in kind of a negative light. I felt like God could've stopped this somehow. I was angry that I had even married Brian. I now saw him as a monster.

Brian moved on in his life and started dating someone else. There was nothing left for me to do, so I filed for divorce. Even though it still broke the little bit of heart I had left, I knew I had to. My children were getting a version of their mother they didn't deserve. I was seeing my children cry frequently about what had happened to mommy and daddy. The pain of it all was too much, and I decided I was going to end my life.

But to Die Is Gain

My life had hit rock bottom. I could not stand the pain anymore and then seeing my three children in pain was more than I could handle. I had decided that the pain in my heart was just too much to bear.

Although I couldn't bear the thought of never seeing my children again, I couldn't bear seeing them hurting like they were. As selfish as some may think suicide is, when you are in that moment, you feel like your death will do everyone else a favor. It was a complete lie of the devil. At that moment the lie was all I could hear and believe.

I had been taking an antidepressant prescribed for me by my doctor. I had been on this certain one for several years. I called the pharmacy that day and had them refill my monthly prescription. Brian was going to be picking up the kids that day, so I asked him if he would pick up my prescription for me and he agreed.

I had already decided when he left with the children I was going to overdose on my antidepressants. So, I looked on the Internet to see how many pills I would need to take to end my life. I didn't want to take too little and just injure myself. I wanted to end it.

After everything I had read, a full bottle of thirty pills should work. Let me remind you, I am not a suicidal person. This was the enemy doing everything he could to get rid of me, even by death. He doesn't care, he wants to bring anyone he can to hell with him. And I was included in that number.

After Brian stopped by the house, he gave me my prescription, got the kids and they were on their way. I was finally alone. I went into the kitchen to get the bottle, opened the lid and to my surprise there were only five pills in the bottle. I was very confused to say the least.

I had been on this certain antidepressant for about three years and never had I received only five pills when having my prescription refilled. I was in disbelief.

When Brian arrived back with our kids, I asked him if he had filled my prescription or not. He told me the pharmacist said my medication was on backorder and they could only give me 5 pills today. In all my three years of being on this medication, it had never ever been on backorder.

God knew my plans! He knew the lie the enemy had fed me. He knew I was going to overdose, and He stopped it. God was watching out for me that day. He was not going to allow the enemy to fulfill his plan for my life. That day, God saved my life. God saved my life!

God didn't only save my life that day, He saved the life of my kids too. They didn't have to go through the pain of losing a mother. And God saved my husband's life too.

A couple days after my suicide decision had been stopped, Brian let me in on a little secret he had. He told me a couple days before I had decided to end my life that he had tried to do the same. He had been staying with his parents during our separation time and decided he was in too much pain for all the pain he was causing.

He was hurt watching what he had done to our children and to me. His pain was different than mine, but it was still pain. He decided he was going to take his own life. He took his grandfather's gun that was fully loaded and went out behind an old shed at his parent's house. He put the gun under his chin and pulled the trigger. The gun didn't fire!

He stood there in confusion because the gun should have fired. He then pointed the gun at the sky and pulled the trigger. This time it fired. He fell to his knees crying because he knew God had stopped the gun from firing. Even while he was right in the middle of his sin, God was still extending to Brian love and mercy. He was calling his son back home.

My attempt at suicide was a turning point for me. I knew God saved my life. The pharmacy didn't know my plans to end my life that day, but God did. He knew what the enemy was planning, and He stepped in to stop it. I owe Him my life. I knew that then and I know it now. I am forever grateful and in awe of Him.

This led me to a road of repentance. I knew I was wrong for turning away from Him and for blaming Him for what the enemy had done. I needed Him more now than at any time of my life. The lie of the enemy is to get you to look at God as the cause of the bad things that happened in our lives. It's a lie. God doesn't cause those bad things to happen, the devil does. But God can use those bad things that have happened and turn them around and use them for our good.

I know it's hard to believe that God can take a bad situation and use it for our good. He can. At one time I thought— "Why would God stop my suicide attempt?" I just couldn't understand. I had been so angry, so bitter, and blamed Him for what had happened. Why wouldn't He just let me go?

> *Luke 5:31–32 (NASB)—And Jesus answered and said to them, "It is not those who are well who need a physician, but those who are sick. I have not come to call the righteous but sinners to repentance."*

I was sick. Sick with a disease called sin. I needed a doctor to help me with this sickness of anger, bitterness, and rage. The list could go on and on. I met with the doctor that day, Doctor Jesus.

The good thing is that He is always in and always available. You don't have to have an appointment. Just meet Him wherever you are, on your knees. That is where I met with Him that day. I asked Him to forgive me for allowing the enemy to poison me.

I asked Him to forgive me for allowing anger to consume me and ruin my life. I asked Him to forgive me for blaming Him, for being angry with Him. God is a big God. He can forgive even the biggest of sins. There is nothing too big or impossible in our thoughts for Him to forgive.

> *1 John 1:9 (NASB)—If we confess our sins, He is faithful and righteous to forgive us our sins and to cleanse us from all unrighteousness.*

I'm not saying that I didn't have a right to be angry because that would be impossible in this situation. However, the anger I had was a very ungodly anger. It consumed my thoughts, my dreams, and the things I talked about.

I was even snapping at the people around me because I was just angry all the time. When I asked Jesus to forgive me and help me with this, He did. It didn't go away overnight, but as I submitted to the Lord and prayed, He slowly started removing anger and replaced it with peace. For me, I had to pray a lot. I felt the most peace in God's presence so that is where I spent a lot of my time. In His presence, He makes all things new. It's just what He does.

This time after about six months of Brian and I being separated, I filed for divorce and things were pretty much on track for being over for good this time. There was a hearing coming up soon to discuss custody arrangements. I was done, he was done, and we were both moving on in our lives.

Then suddenly, out of nowhere, Brian started coming around the house a lot more than normal. He mostly stayed away because seeing the kids hurt. It hurt him too much, so he thought if he stayed away, he would hurt less, and they would too.

That doesn't work. It only made the times he did come around more painful for everyone. However, he started coming over to the house more. He wanted to be around the children and I. Day after day after day he would come over and spend time with us.

I was very leery. I could see in his eyes he was missing his family. But of course, him leaving over and over and then wanting to return had become a common occurrence.

I am convinced that saying about the "grass being greener on the other side" is a lie. I think the grass on the other side is Astro Turf. Brian would leave and get his taste of the world, of what he thought he wanted. Then he realized that wasn't what he wanted. He discovered that the enemy had fooled him yet again.

What I didn't know was that the Lord had been working on his heart for weeks. He had started severing the connection with the girl he was with at that time. And he started coming to church with the kids and I on Sundays. Then again this was common occurrence as well.

When Brian wanted to return, he would always put his best foot forward, wanting me to believe he was a 'changed' man and that I could trust him again. I didn't know what to do. This was all too familiar territory for me. My trust was completely gone. I didn't know if that was something I could even get back again. And if I did, would it be ripped away again?

However, something inside me kept telling me to give him one more chance. That something was God. "But Lord, You know what he has done and what he is capable of doing. Why would you ask me to take him back? I can't trust him anymore and we will both be miserable like before."

This was just one of the many questions I had for the Lord when I felt he was asking me to receive Brian back. I really wanted to have my family back together but at what price? My children had already been exposed to so much garbage from Brian and me. I was afraid history would only repeat itself. My children didn't need that again. I didn't need that again. So here I am faced with a decision: Do I allow him to return home, or do I call it quits?

CHAPTER 7

Strength for One More Day

After a considerable amount of praying, I decided to let Brian come back home. The decision wasn't easy; however, I knew it was what the Lord was telling me to do. Despite my fears, doubt, uncertainty, and with little to no hope, I agreed to try one last time.

Letting him come back home again was very hard for me. My nerves were on edge with every little thing. I was staking everything on what I felt God had told me to do. This was hard because I was still unclear if I was hearing God correctly. Hearing the voice of God has not always been the easiest thing for me, so to place a big decision on 'thinking this is God' was very scary. Nevertheless, I went through with what I thought was right.

It was a very unpopular decision to say the least. My family was my biggest support and to see Brian back in the home was not okay with them. And they made it known to me. They were very concerned as were many close friends. No one wanted to see my children, or me hurt again.

Of course, this was also my biggest concern. Was I putting my children back in harm's way by allowing a habitual abandoner back into their lives? I fully understood why they were so concerned. Sometimes, though, God will ask you to do what's unpopular. And it may be unpopular to your own sense of understanding.

According to our usual pattern, we decided to start up marriage counseling again. I do have to say that we had the best marriage counselor ever.

When Brian would leave she'd stay by my side through it all. Moreover, when Brian would come back home, she never treated him like he deserved. Instead, she was kind and showed him mercy. She was truly an example of what a true follower of Christ should be.

At the very beginning of this time of reconciliation, I was being attacked relentlessly in my mind by the enemy. Satan will bombard your mind with all kinds of tormenting images if you let him.

When I went to sleep, my dreams were plagued with dreams of him with other women. I couldn't even find peace in sleeping. I couldn't figure out what to do, who to turn to, or who to help me.

I had this deep aching sore in my heart and all I desperately wanted was someone, anyone to help me. No one in my family had gone through adultery before. No one could understand this immense pain I was feeling all the time.

I felt like my life was caving in on me and there was nothing I could do to stop it. The pain was too great and the betrayal too deep. I couldn't see a way out of this abyss. "Lord, help me," was my nightly prayer. *Lord, help me*!

That also became my daily prayer. And I let Him help me. I had so many conflicting emotions. One minute I was dealing with pain from the past, then I'd be dealing with various fears, and then I'd dare to be optimistic about the future.

Even though I was severely wounded and couldn't visualize how things could work out, I still had hope that all would be well. Essentially my hope was mixed with fear. I was constantly hoping for the best but feared the worst. What a hard place to continually be living in!

I loved someone that I hated at the same time and then was trying to trust someone I couldn't trust because that had been severed many times. I was trying to work through a situation that appeared virtually impossible.

Every day I wondered if I had made the right decision. Will this really be different, or will I be reliving the past and causing my children and myself more pain? My only peace in this situation was when I would go to the Lord in prayer. Each time He would refill me with His peace and His love.

The only problem was that I seemed to be having a hard time sustaining that peace and love with me through the day. Some days as soon as I walked out of my prayer time, all the gloom, despair, and hopelessness were right there waiting for me.

I really tried with everything I could to work my way out of this. It felt like I was locked in my bedroom, screaming at the top of my lungs and no noise was coming out.

In addition, my heart was laid open in this locked bedroom and bleeding profusely; yet nothing or nobody could stop the pain. It was one of the loneliest times of my life.

And the enemy took advantage of my situation and I was overwhelmingly consumed with dark thoughts. Since I felt so lonely then I felt that no one did or even could understand my pain.

I tried to go to Brian for help, but I knew he couldn't help me. He would try, but there was only so much he could do. I really wanted him to help; however, at the same time, I would see him as the perpetrator. It's like trying to find solace in someone who raped you.

After all, he was the one who caused the pain so why couldn't he help me get rid of it? At least that was how I viewed it. Truthfully, he was helping me tremendously by doing everything in his power to help me feel secure.

He allowed me to put a tracking device on his cell phone without complaint and tried the best he could to keep himself transparent and accountable. Somehow it wasn't enough for me. This is just a small glimpse into the emotional roller coaster I was on during that time.

For several months I looked for help outside of the Lord. I needed a tangible fix. I wanted to be able to feel something instantly. The only thing I didn't realize was that the problem wasn't created instantly; therefore, there was a good chance the fix wouldn't be instant either.

I tried talking through emotions with my family and close friends. Now that was a major problem. I was still very hurt and angry with him and so were they. And because of that they couldn't listen or offer advice objectively. As a matter of fact, our conversations would start out good and were very helpful; then ever so slowly it proceeded to assassinating my husband's character.

I was angry and miserable. And misery loves company. Moreover, misery seeks out like-minded company. When someone agrees with you, it almost makes you feel better and justified. I wanted these like-minded people to hop on my bandwagon and be my cheerleader.

As terrible as that sounds, it happens every day and in many different situations. Satan himself is miserable and seeks to make everyone else miserable along with him.

> **Ephesians 4:29 (NASB)—Let no unwholesome word proceed from your mouth, but only such a word as is good for edification according to the need of the moment, so that it will give grace to those who hear it.**

This was just another attempt to ease the pain. Sometimes I would think if I could 'get it all out' then it would all 'be out'. In my thinking, I just needed to talk about my problem and somehow get all my emotions out.

In doing this, I hoped and prayed all the hurt, pain, and betrayal would disappear. Well, that doesn't work! By the time I was finished talking out my problems, I ended up being angrier than when I first started.

This is what happened when I went looking for outside ways to heal my heart. They were temporary fixes for the moment. The Lord is the only permanent healer of your heart. He is the only one who can make the wrongs right and bring justice. Only He alone can do it.

> **Psalms 147: 3 (NASB)—He heals the brokenhearted and binds up their wounds.**

I was wounded and in need of a healer. I had so many good friends who stood beside me during this difficult time. Strangely enough, one of those who stood by me was my husband.

Before, when Brian would come back home, I would think that things will start looking positive; however, quite the opposite occurred. When you are wounded as severely as I was, you will start looking at everything through a lens of suspicion.

You start seeing everything as a *potential to harm you*. It doesn't just happen in your home; you start seeing the outside world through this lens as well. Everything you see becomes tainted. You begin to build walls that are so high it makes it almost impossible for someone to scale. What's worse is that it makes it harder for you to climb over as well.

This protective fort I built around myself was a device the enemy used to keep my hurt protected and unhealed. Now that I am hidden within my walls I can continue to be watchful by looking through my lens of suspicion. I had become a professional victim and everyone else was seen as a suspect.

Brian was different the last time he came back because the Lord had done something in him. The Lord had transformed him. What I didn't know was, while he was away, the Lord was working behind the scenes. Brian was having a series of dreams which was causing him great distress. He later told me he was having dreams of people he greatly respected approaching him on a road telling him "Brian, what are you doing? It's time to turn around!" But the straw that broke the camel's back was the nightmare he had of our daughter. He dreamed that our daughter was in hell screaming "Daddy, save me"! He woke up weeping and continued the rest of that night. He knew he needed to change and needed to return to God. He knew his behaviors were going to lead our children down a road he could not bear to even think about. He changed this time, for good.

I was having a hard time believing and trusting. Even though I could sense something was "different", I still didn't trust that it was true. Previously, whenever he would come back home, I had a long list of things he was not allowed to do with a longer list of consequences. I felt that if I could box him in with rules and consequences, I would safeguard myself that way. Well, that didn't work.

I do believe that when trust is broken it must be rebuilt, but the way I went about it was very wrong. My thoughts had to do with controlling, not rebuilding. There is a difference. When you rebuild, it is done together. Control is one person dominating the other.

The actual definition of control is the power to influence or direct people's behavior or the course of events. My thought was that if he just does what I say, he wouldn't hurt me again. Frankly, it's just a form of control. Control does not work and does not promote a loving relationship in any situation.

When he came home, I decided that I was not going the control route anymore. It only made me miserable and it didn't work anyway and only made me feel crazy. I determined I was going to give Brian to God. Yes, I gave him back to God.

I gave up the control and handed him over to God. That's a very difficult thing to do. Many times, I would have to do it daily. I would tell the Lord, "I know I gave Brian to You yesterday, but I'm going to give him to You again today."

Making the choice to give Brian to God everyday helped me to finally relinquish control, which allowed God to move. The Lord brought a conviction to Brian's heart that in my best attempt I never could.

It was a real conviction, a fear of the Lord that no human can create. It also came with a loving fear for the Lord. When

God comes in and meets you right in the middle of your sin, it changes you. What just amazes me about the God I serve is that He isn't repulsed by our sins.

In fact, our sin draws Him to us. He loves us so much He wants to set us free from our sin. He doesn't want us to live in it any longer. He wants us to leave the road the enemy has laid out and free us from all sin and death.

We are why He sent His Son, Jesus. Now we can go to the Father to ask forgiveness for our sins and we are forgiven. Jesus paid the price thousands of years ago. He was the atoning sacrifice for us; therefore, our sins are forgiven. When I say God is attracted to our sin, I mean He is drawn to the sinner because His heart desires to set us free.

> *Romans 3:23 (NASB)—for all have sinned and fall short of the glory of God,*

> *1 John 1:9 (NASB)—If we confess our sins, He is faithful and righteous to forgive us our sins and to cleanse us from all unrighteousness.*

He is an amazing God who loves us with an amazing love. It is a love that cannot be replicated and one that totally satisfies. It is not like the love we experience in the world, that love is temporal.

The love that comes from God the Father is a love that will not leave you lacking or wanting more. It is complete in all form. It completes you. He completes you.

Only the Lord can fill all those empty places we have in our hearts from the cares and hurts of the world. And He'll fill you to overflowing. The love He has shown to you, now you can show to others. This love God gives is totally undeserved.

We don't have to work hard to attain it. We don't have to do a long list of deeds to feel worthy of it. His love is just there. It's for all of us. It's unconditional and unafraid of all of our mess. His love goes to those places no one sees but us. Those places we hide because if anyone knew what we were really like, they would turn their back on us. God's love goes there to those places and isn't repulsed. It's undeserved love and so complete. Amazing!

Since Christ loves me with an undeserving love, then why do I not show my husband the same love? If being a Christian means to be Christ-like, doesn't that mean in every way?

It shouldn't be just the ones I pick and choose to do. Christ's love forgives all, endures all, hopes, and rejoices with good. It never ceases! 1 Corinthians 13 is the perfect example of what true love is all about. We are to extend to extend this type of love to everyone, even those who have hurt us. Maybe, just maybe He is saying, "Love others, especially those who have hurt you. It's hard to do, but it's can be done.

1 Corinthians 13:4–8 (NASB)—
Love is patient, love is kind and is not jealous; love does not brag and is not arrogant, does not act unbecomingly; it does not seek its own, is not provoked, does not take into account a wrong suffered, does not rejoice in unrighteousness, but rejoices with the truth; bears all things, believes all things, hopes all things, endures all things. Love never fails.

I think I have broken about every example that the Bible says love really is. We are all learning. If you are alive and breathing today, you are still learning. God knows we will not get it right every day; however, He encourages us to strive towards this standard of love.

Jesus gave us the example of love in its most perfect form. He knew beforehand we would turn our back on Him. He knew we would hurt His heart with all our sin, and then do it again and again. He knew all of this in advance and still He went to the cross.

How many of us can say we would die for someone knowing in advance they would take our death for granted and treat it as nothing? I think it's safe to say not one of us would. That is exactly what Jesus did for us.

He gave us grace, showing love when love is undeserved. So how can I not show my husband the same love? How can I withhold forgiveness when Christ has forgiven me for so much? Am I saying that my hurt is just too deep and too unforgivable?

No! If Jesus can forgive me for my multitude of sins, I can forgive Brian for his. If I am truly a Christian, then I must do just as Jesus does: love and forgive.

I desperately needed Him to help me heal. After countless tries, I knew this was something I could not do on my own. I needed this healer of my heart.

> *Isaiah 40:31 (NASB)—Yet those who wait for the Lord, will gain new strength; they will mount up with wings like eagles, they will run and not get tired, they will walk and not become weary.*

> *Isaiah 41:10 (NASB)—'Do not fear, for I am with you; Do not anxiously look about you, for I am your God. I will strengthen you, surely I will help you, Surely I will uphold you with My righteous right hand'.*

There are many scriptures about the Lord being our strength but when you are in the midst of pain how do you do that? And what does that look like: letting the Lord be my strength?

God is my stronghold, He is my support and assistance, to help me overcome my enemies, and he is my source of strength in danger. To acknowledge God, as my strength doesn't mean I just simply say it with my mouth, it is something I must choose to live by constantly staying in the word of God and praying throughout the day. Therefore, I cannot afford to go one day without spending time with the Lord. He gives me the strength I need for that day and the strength for the battles ahead.

Forgiveness Is Not a
Feeling...it is a Choice!

So, if I decide I am going to forgive, all the pain goes away with that decision, right? Wrong! Forgiveness is not a feeling, at first anyway. It is a choice. I had to make a choice every day that I was going to forgive Brian.

I knew on this journey of forgiveness I would be walking through some painful situations, but I knew the Lord was going to be right there with me. He will never ask you to walk somewhere He has not already been. He knows pain and He knows how it feels to be rejected. We do it to Him every day.

When you feel that tug at your heart to go spend time with the Lord and you decide to watch TV instead, you have just said, "Lord, the TV means more to me right now than time with You." I have done this time and time again, sad to say. If our spouse wanted to spend time with us just talking and we turned them down to watch TV or do something else, we would injure the other's feelings. We wouldn't do that to our spouses, but we will do it to the Lord all the time. Still, He loves us, desires us, accepts us, and continually draws us to come to Him, just as we are.

> *Colossians 3:13 (NASB)—Bearing with one another, and forgiving each other, whoever has a complaint against anyone; just as the Lord forgave you, so also should you.*

> *Matthew 18:21–22 (NASB)— Then Peter came and said to Him, "Lord, how often shall my brother sin against me and I forgive him? Up to seven times?" Jesus said to him, "I do not say to you, up to seven times, but up to seventy times seven."*

Seventy-seven times? Yes, that is what the Bible says. We should forgive someone who sins against us seventy-seven times daily. Other translations say: seventy times seven, which means four hundred and ninety times. That is a lot of forgiving each day.

Jesus is telling us to forgive in the verse because forgiveness will keep us from becoming bitter. Forgiveness sets us free. It's not so much for the other person as it is for us. Not forgiving someone is like being held in a jail cell.

When we forgive a person, who has wronged us or caused us pain, it's as if we have opened the jail cell to our freedom. Forgiveness does not mean we're saying it's all right what the other person has done to us by any means. It just releases us from being a prisoner all our lives to bitterness.

Our freedom is why Jesus commands us to forgive. By forgiving, we are no longer shackled in the chains of bitterness and anger the enemy would like to keep us in. There is freedom through forgiveness!

> *John 8: 32 (NASB)—And you will know the truth, and the truth will make you free."*

The devil doesn't know what to do when we forgive. It goes against everything he believes. In fact, forgiveness is something he can't figure out how to combat. Forgiveness = Freedom. He would like to keep us trapped and tangled up in bitterness.

It's not enough for him to have people do terrible things to us, but he wants to keep us trapped in the hurt of the action he created to begin with. The choice to truly forgive busts down walls that were built, frees the captive, and brings joy to the heart.

Forgiving is definitely a life changer; however, it is not easy. Forgiveness is a daily conscious choice I had to make every day even when I wasn't feeling like I wanted to. Many times, I had to remind myself that I chose to forgive him. Forgiveness is not a scapegoat for the other person either.

> *John 8:1–11 (NASB)—But Jesus went to the Mount of Olives. Early in the morning He came into the temple, and all the people were coming to Him; and He sat down and began to teach them. The scribes and the Pharisees*

brought a woman caught in adultery and having set her in the center of the court, they said to Him, "Teacher, this woman has been caught in adultery, in the very act. Now in the Law of Moses commanded us to stone such a woman; what then do You say?" They were saying this, testing Him, so that they might have grounds for accusing Him. But Jesus stopped down and with His finger wrote on the ground. But when they persisted in asking Him, He straightened up, and said to them, "He who is without sin among you, let him be the first to throw a stone at her." Again, He stooped down and wrote on the ground. When they heard it, they began to go out one by one, beginning with the older ones, and He was left alone, and the woman, where she was, in the center of the court. Straightening up, Jesus said to her, "Woman, where are they? Did no one condemn you?" She said, "No one, Lord." And Jesus said, "I do not condemn you, either. Go. From now on sin no more."

Jesus addresses the sinner and the sin in John 8. He forgives the woman caught in adultery (the sinner) but commands her to go and sin no more. He is giving her direction as to what she must do after being forgiven. She is not to sin any more. She must lay the sin down and pick up righteousness in its place.

Personally, forgiveness took a long time. Somedays I even wondered if I had even forgiven because I still felt so angry and fearful most of the time. Yes, you read correctly, my anger had now given way to fear and in a very big way.

I was so afraid of the past repeating itself. I was afraid of getting hurt and my children being hurt again. My fear had compounded to the point that it had become this massive thing in my life. Basically, I lived under a blanket of fear, which is no life at all.

God had brought my family back together. Now the enemy was trying to keep me imprisoned in the fear of the past and the fear of 'what if' for the future. It was a miserable place to be.

My husband was trying very hard to make me feel secure by being as transparent as he could be with me. He was doing everything I asked of him. He was giving me no reason to fear the future, but I was still extremely fearful.

I was allowing the enemy to torment me with the thoughts of the past and had vain imaginations of what will happen in the future. In other words, I started believing and acting as if things that had not happened yet already did. My fear was crippling.

The enemy is not content with just splitting apart your family. In his own sinister way, he wants to take everyone out individually. He is conniving, relentless, and wants to take everyone he can to hell with him.

> *1 Peter 5:8 (NASB)—Be of sober spirit, be on the alert. Your adversary, the devil, prowls around like a roaring lion, seeking someone to devour.*

This verse tells me that the devil is always looking, always seeking out someone to take down and devour. When Peter wrote this, wild lions still roamed parts of the Middle East. A wild lion, like Satan, is deceptive. They are great hunters that do most of their work at night.

Their tan coats are a natural camouflage that blends in with their surroundings well. This helps them to stalk their prey. The lion likes to creep slowly towards its victim behind the cover of tall grasses.

They are selective hunters. They attack the stragglers, the old, the sick, and the young. They will strike into the pack if necessary, but they prefer everything in their favor.

Can you see why Peter compared Satan to a lion? The great deceiver, more often than not, works under cover of darkness. He patiently stalks his prey and is invisible to them. His night vision is sharp. And his senses are much sharper than ours. He is always looking for a way to maneuver us into a position where we are by ourselves.

At this time of my life I was an easy target for the enemy. I was sick with hurt, angry, bitter, resentfulness, and fearfulness. I was a big mixture of everything the enemy loves to do to people in my situation.

Forgiveness is very hard to do or even think about when the enemy is keeping your past right in front of you. Imagine trying to drive a car but only looking in the rear-view mirror. Before long, you will be in the ditch.

Isaiah 43:18–19 (NASB)—"Do not call to mind the former things or ponder things of the past. "Behold, I will do something new, now it will spring forth; will you not be aware of it? I will even make a roadway in the wilderness, rivers in the desert.

What is the Lord saying in Isaiah 43? Let it go! Don't dwell any longer on those past hurts, those past disappointments, and those past regrets. There is no life in the past. Leave it there.

When I decided to leave the past in the past I truly started the journey of forgiveness with the Lord. I knew it would not be easy, but I also knew it would be worth it all. After all, my desire was for my marriage to be saved.

I did want to see things work out. And my children needed and deserved to have the best version of their parents they could. I just didn't know how to get there. This journey of forgiveness was not easy, but well worth it. It all started with: I choose to forgive you.

I choose to no longer be a prisoner to my mind and to the past. I choose to let you heal me Lord. I choose! The Lord never forces us to do anything that we do not want to do. He is very patient with us and lets us arrive at that place when we are ready.

When we are finally ready to lay it all down at his feet. This means we give Him all our cares, all our worries, and all our fears. He wants to and will take everything that holds us back from Him.

Forgiveness is something I have had to learn and what better teacher than the one who knows forgiveness best. The actual definition of forgiveness is the action or process of forgiving or being forgiven. This tells me that forgiveness is not something that just happens. It is an action and a process.

It was a process with me. I did not get it right every time either. Allow yourself some grace, we all make mistakes and are learning as we go along. There were many times the enemy would come around with a tormenting thought about the past.

At first, I would grab that thought and attach it to an emotion or hurt I had, and it was all over at that point. Once I started to realize those tormenting thoughts were not my own and I did not have to allow them to torment me, that was a game changer for me. When I realized I could command those thoughts to go, they would go.

> *2 Corinthians 10: 4–5 (NASB)—*
> *For the weapons of our warfare are not of the flesh, but divinely powerful for the destruction of fortresses. We are destroying speculations and every lofty thing raised up against the knowledge of God, and we are taking every thought captive to the obedience of Christ.*

I needed to know what it meant to 'bring every thought into captivity'. The enemy was set on attacking my mind, so I needed to know what I had to do. After all, this is a spiritual battle. In this kind of battle, we do not war in the flesh to bring the victory. It is important to remember who the enemy is and where your battle lines are drawn. Our flesh is powerless against the enemy.

Being a Christian in this world means not doing battle the way the world does battle. God helps us. He helps us, His children, to love our enemies and at the same time we are tearing down sinful ways of thinking.

Since every thought is to be brought into captivity to Christ, we should bring every thought that does not line up with God's word and examine it under the light of the word. When you do this, you will know if the thought is from God or from Satan. Essentially, the thoughts we give 'life' to will gain life. Therefore, we must pick and choose the thoughts we'll listen to. We decide! It's all a choice.

Life is all about choices. We decide to forgive or to not forgive, to lose weight or to not lose weight, to clean the house or leave it a mess. Everything is a choice, a decision. It includes what we do spiritually as well. God will never force His ideas, His perspective or anything else on us. He wants us to choose Him for ourselves.

Over the years I have discovered that I was always coming to Him in my moments of crisis. I'd come to Him, begging Him to just take the pain away. Take the sadness away, Lord. Please, take it all from me!

He was the one I went to in my moments of anger and rage. I would shake my fist at heaven screaming "Why me?" He never turned me away and He never looked the other away either. He was always right there, and I knew He was there because His peace would just overtake me during those times.

At times when my anger was just raging like a fire inside me I would get in the presence of the Lord and the anger would leave. His peace would replace the anger I felt. When I was afraid, I would get in his presence and all fear would be gone. God is a good Father that will never leave us the way we come to Him.

Forgiveness is complicated, both in serious situations like mine and in everyday situations. When you have been deeply hurt, the idea of forgiving may feel like you're being asked to tear your heart out and give it to the very person who trampled on it in the first place.

In these difficult situations, we sometimes put a burden on ourselves. We think if we forgive, we must completely forgive and get over it immediately. Remember, forgiveness is a process, not a one-time act. It begins with the decision to forgive, and it may take time before the heart fully accepts the request we have made of it.

I believe how long it takes to truly forgive depends on the severity of the pain. We need to give ourselves grace as we move toward complete forgiveness. When we have been deeply wronged, something inside us yearns for justice and if we don't forgive, our desire for justice turns to revenge. Revenge is a very dangerous place to be. Revenge is when you want the other person to 'feel your pain'.

True forgiveness takes place when we release our hurt and let go of it, knowing that our spouse (and me included) is a fallen human being. We are all fallen people in need of a Savior.

Ephesians 4:32 (NASB)—Be kind to one another, tender-hearted, forgiving each other, just as God in Christ also has forgiven you.

Matthew 6:14 (NASB)—For if you forgive others for their transgressions, your heavenly Father will also forgive you.

In the same manner we forgive others, God will forgive us but also in the same manner we do not forgive, the Lord will not forgive us. Forgiveness is not an easy thing, but it is a command of the Lord, and it is worth it.

If there is something in your life, you have not forgiven someone for, I would encourage you today to let it go. Start a journey of forgiveness, not for the other person, but for you.

Where Did It All go Wrong?

Through this process I had a lot of questions: What went wrong? How did all this bad happen to our marriage? I see so many couples that never have anything bad ever happen. They seem to live perfect lives, have perfect houses, drive perfect cars and have perfect children.

Yet here I am with a marriage that is hanging on by a thread, a husband I can barely trust, and children scarred from what we had done to them. What went wrong? When Brian and I got married, we committed our marriage to the Lord. We said these beautiful vows to each other promising to keep God in the center of our marriage. Again, what went wrong?

Ecclesiastes 4:12 (NASB)—...A cord of three strands is not quickly torn apart.

This verse is used so often during wedding ceremonies, but I don't think we fully understand what this verse means.

For a marriage to survive, Jesus needs to be involved in the relationship.

A threefold cord includes the husband and wife being the first two strands. Then they are intertwined with the middle strand that is God. Being united with God gives us the strength to cope with problems and it is the key to achieving the greatest of happiness in marriage.

According to this verse, I would say our problem started right there. We had dedicated our marriage to God in the beginning, but we did not keep it dedicated to God. The middle strand started to be removed. And we were removing that middle strand ourselves. That scripture states that a 3-strand cord is not easily broken, so this must also mean that a 2-strand cord is easily broken. God did not, for one moment, walk away from us. We walked away from Him. And when we did…we removed the 3rd strand.

We both loved God, but I think as our marriage progressed, our love for the world became bigger. We started letting things into our lives we never thought we would. It wasn't something we decided to do, it was a slow fade. It's like getting into a boat and before you know it you've drifted very far from the shore. We never intended for that to happen, but over time, complacency begin to set in and we had drifted very far from the one who could help us.

We decided to start having "fun" in our marriage and this included partying and drinking. I know this can be a touchy subject, but I want to give you my opinion on this subject.

I am coming from a place of experience and seeing the harm it has done in my marriage because we allowed a seemingly harmless thing in, or so we thought. For example, on one occasion my husband and I were attending a party. I was pregnant at the time with our first child; therefore, I did not drink.

My husband, on the other hand, was given the green light to drink by me. Even though something inside of me was uneasy about it, I didn't want to be the one at the party causing 'drama' so I allowed it. He started drinking at the party.

I could see the few drinks he was limiting himself to quickly increased as more and more friends were now in the mix. Before I knew it, he was full blown drunk and the life of the party. He didn't sound like himself or even look like himself. I decided at that point I wanted to leave and told him it was time to go, and I drove us home.

On the way home, I started to become very angry at his drunken state, so I decided I was going to pretend I was a NASCAR driver. I began driving very fast and taking turns at high speeds. Thank the Lord, we didn't wreck, but I did have to pull over, so he could throw up the liquor in his stomach.

This wasn't the best decision I have made in my life. However, now you can understand what the effects of alcohol had on him. He had decided he was only going to have a few; unfortunately, the alcohol blurred that line turning a black/white issue into a hazy gray.

It's in those gray moments we can think things and do things under the control of another 'spirit'. The Bible clearly states to be 'sober' minded and not to get drunk so that we never surrender our body, mind or soul to anything other than God.

Proverbs 20:1 (NASB)—Wine is a mocker, strong drink a brawler, and whoever is intoxicated by it is not wise.

Ephesians 5:15–18 (NASB)— Therefore be careful how you walk, not as unwise men but as wise, making the most of your time, because the days are evil. So then do not be foolish but understand what the will of the Lord is. And do not get drunk with wine, for that is dissipation, but be filled with the Spirit.

The Bible doesn't come right out and say, "Thou shalt not drink beer." However, it does make references to it as being unwise. God is more interested in your heart and motives than he is in drinking.

If drinking becomes a way to escape problems or boost courage, then your faith in God is shaky and your character is probably at risk. When you are living God's purpose, then alcohol isn't required for a good time and your life will show by your good fruit.

Galatians 5:22–23(NASB)—But the fruit of the Spirit is love, joy, peace, patience, kindness, goodness, faithfulness, gentleness, self-control; against such things there is no law.

In our home, alcohol never produced anything positive. Any memory I have that involved alcohol always has a negative undertone attached to it. It is the same way for my husband. He has many more stories he could share on the terrible road he went down and how alcohol was a close friend during that time. I guess my question is: Can you find joy, truth, and integrity without it?

When we allowed alcohol abuse into our marriage, it opened a door in our souls for the enemy to come right in.

We have many gateways or doors to our soul. These are also known as entry points for the devil to come into our lives, homes, and relationships.

> *Revelation 3:20 (NASB)—Behold, I stand at the door and knock; if anyone hears My voice and opens the door, I will come in to him and will dine with him, and he with Me.*

Some of the gateways the enemy uses as an entry point into our lives are touch, taste, smell, sight and hearing, our five senses. Understanding what a gateway is can be a little confusing.

A gateway is a place of authority where control is exercised. Whoever controls your different gateways has authority and control over you. Without realizing it, we may have given demons access and control to sit in those gateways and dominate. It's a scary thing to think that something we allow into our life could ultimately have control over us.

> *Romans 12:2 (NASB)—And do not be conformed to this world, but be transformed by the renewing of your mind, so that you may prove what the will of God is, that which is good and acceptable and perfect.*

> *1 Corinthians 6:12 (NASB)—All things are lawful for me, but not all things are profitable. All things are lawful for me, but I will not be mastered by anything.*

Whatever we allow into our lives, we essentially are giving a part of ourselves away to. We both fell prey to pornography. This is not something that just men struggle with, but women also.

We both dabbled in it to some extent. And in doing so, we gave the enemy access to the gateway of our sight. Once this gateway is defiled, a strong spirit of lust can sit right over the gateway. Once a person has opened their life to pornography at the sight gate, they will continually be pulled back because the demon wants to see more.

Therefore, people continually fall back into pornography. There is a constant pull to see more. It is something we must pray to Jesus to have removed. It can be removed, and you can be set free from this demonic hold.

> *1 Corinthians 6:18–20 (NASB)—*
> *Flee immorality. Every other sin that a man commits is outside the body, but immoral man sins against his own body. Or do you not know that your body is the temple of the Holy Spirit who is in you, whom you have from God, and that you are not your own? For you have been bought with a price: therefore, glorify God in your body.*

The Bible even gives us clear instruction of what is not from God.

> *1 John 2:15–16 (NASB)—Do not love the world nor the things in the world. If anyone loves the world, the love of the Father is not in him. For all*

*that is in the world, the lust of the flesh
and the lust of the eyes and the boastful
pride of life, is not from the Father but
is from the world.*

If the eyes, ears, nose, and mouth, are gateways to our soul, this means they are a point of entry for either the Holy Spirit or the devil. Brian and I did not do a very good job of guarding our gateways. In fact, we allowed just about anything to come in and take over that area. I can't count the number of times we have said, "If we only knew then, what we know now."

Pornography is a slippery slope of ever-increasing wickedness. The three main categories of sin are: the lust of the flesh, the lust of the eyes, and the pride of life (1 John 2:16).

Pornography causes us to lust after flesh, and it is undeniably a lust of the eyes. It is addictive, destructive, and offensive to God. For those involved in pornography, God can and will give the victory. The first step is to confess your sin to God.

*1 John 1:9 (NASB)—If we confess
our sins, He is faithful and righteous
to forgive us our sins and to cleanse us
from all unrighteousness.*

Ask God to cleanse, renew, and transform your mind.

*Romans 12:2 (NASB)—And do
not be conformed to this world, but be
transformed by the renewing of your
mind, so that you may prove what the*

will of God is, that which is good and acceptable and perfect.

Ask God to fill your mind with:

Philippians 4:8 (NASB)—Finally, brethren, whatever is true, whatever is honorable, whatever is right, whatever is pure, whatever is lovely, whatever is of good repute, if there is any excellence and if anything, worthy of praise, dwell on these things.

Galatians 5:16 (NASB)—But I say, walk by the Spirit, and you will not carry out the desire of the flesh.

Pornography is something the Lord can help you get free from, but you must make the decision that you want to be free. God will not just take it from you, but if you want help, He will help you get free.

Brian and I made so many bad choices to allow harmful things into our marriage early on. We didn't stand by our decision to keep God at the center of our marriage. Instead, we allowed the enemy to come in and wreak havoc in our home.

Our desires for the world became bigger than our desires for God, and because of that, our marriage paid a big price. With sin, there is always a price tag. In God there is safety and in God there is protection.

The further from God you get, the less protection you have. A good example would be a fire. The closer you are to the fire, the more you can feel the warmth of its flames.

However, the further you get from the fire, the less of its warmth you feel and the further into the darkness you become.

When you take God out of the number one spot in your life, He becomes number two, then number three and before you know it, He doesn't even make the list anymore. We had removed God from the number one spot.

Psalms 46:1 (NASB)—God is our refuge and strength, a very present help in trouble.

God is always present and always willing to help us. I believe that most of the time, we don't ask Him for His help. We try to do life on our own and in our own way. We have this mentality of "I can do this on my own."

Sometimes it's because we don't want to feel like a burden. Sometimes we don't want to be turned down, and sometimes we just want to control everything. There is nothing wrong with seeking help. In fact, God wants to help us.

He wants to be asked. We need to ask Him for help daily because we won't get far in life trying to live off our own strength. Believing that we can do everything on our own, will only lead to failure.

Sometimes God helps us by doing things Himself and sometimes God helps us through other people. Asking for help doesn't mean you're weak, it actually means you are strong and wise.

Isaiah 41:10 (NASB)—Do not fear, for I am with you; do not anxiously look about you, for I am your God. I will strengthen you, surely, I will

help you, surely, I will uphold you with
My righteous right hand.

Not only will He help us, but He will also strengthen us if we ask Him. We had allowed many things into our marriage, many toxic things that seemed all right to the outside world. We believed the lie: what did it really hurt, right?

We did whatever we wanted and didn't give much thought to it otherwise. We didn't see it as "harming" ourselves, but simply making ourselves happy. We still went to church most Sundays which helped us compensate for our lifestyle. We wanted to make sure we had our "Sunday attendance" card punched every Sunday. We still played the part like we had it all together.

We stood alongside each other, raising our hands, unaware of what we were doing to our marriage and ourselves. We were unaware that the things we were doing at that time was hurting our future children. We were also unaware that the things we were doing then actually had a price to it.

Sin always has a price. It just hides the price tag from you. You think you are the only one affected, the only one who really sees and really knows. What a lie! The things you do, do not only affect you.

Nothing is ever hidden. Sin always has a way of coming to the surface; including those secret sins you think will never be found or uncovered. God will not let the sin stay hidden. It's because He loves us that He exposes it. He exposes what it is doing to us. He doesn't do it to embarrass us, but to help us. Sin is costly. It costs your life. God exposes your sin because He is merciful. Because He is good!

Romans 6:23 (NASB)—For the
wages of sin is death, but the free gift

of God is eternal life in Christ Jesus our Lord.

Jesus died on the cross and paid that death penalty for us. He did that knowing some of us would never come to know Him or accept what He did for us, but He did it anyway. I don't know anyone that loves me that much, knowing fully that I may not ever acknowledge what was done for me, yet decide to die for me anyway.

It is a love I don't think I will ever understand. It's totally undeserved, but it is what it is, pure love, undeserved, unashamed, and available for us every day. His love doesn't change, isn't put off by our sin, doesn't run from us, and doesn't leave us. It's always looking, always pursuing and never quitting.

Love is why He can't leave us in our sin. If you saw your child running out into oncoming traffic, you would do everything you could to stop them. God tries to do that for us. He knows what sin does. It separates us from Him; therefore, He does everything to try to get us to turn around and come back to Him.

He is a loving Father and He will put roadblocks in our way to slow us down. He wants us to see the truth of what is really going on. He doesn't want us to fall away and die not knowing Him and then be eternally separated. God is forgiving, loving, and full of mercy. He extends mercy to us over and over and over again. He offers mercy more times than we would ever consider giving.

We have this mentality of always looking out for ourselves. Someone hurts us, and we're determined that they won't get the chance to hurt us again. We'll cut that person out of our lives and build up walls. As a result, we let people in only so close because we no longer trust people.

I'm thankful God is not that way. I have let Him down time after time and yet each time I come back to Him, His arms are wide open. And He doesn't list my faults. Instead, He is lovingly ready to accept me back home.

Luke 15:11–24 (NASB)—And He said, "A man had two sons. The younger of them said to his father, 'Father, give me my share of the estate that falls to me.' So, he divided his wealth between them. And not many days later, the younger son gathered everything together and went on a journey into a distant country, and there he squandered his estate with loose living. Now when he had spent everything, a severe famine occurred in that country, and he began to be impoverished. So, he went and hired himself out to one of the citizens of that country, and he sent him into his fields to feed swine. And he would have gladly filled his stomach with the pods that the swine were eating, and no one was giving anything to him. But when he came to his senses, he said, 'How many of my father's hired men have more than enough bread, but I am dying here with hunger! I will get up and go to my father, and will say to him, "Father, I have sinned against heaven, and in your sight; I am no longer worthy to be called your son; make me as one of your hired me."' So, he got

up and came to his father. But while he
was still a long way off, his father saw
him and felt compassion for him, and
ran and embraced him and kissed him,
'Father, I have sinned against heaven
and in your sight; I am no longer wor-
thy to be called your son.' But the father
said to his slaves, 'Quickly bring out the
best robe and put it on him and put
a ring on his hand and sandals on his
feet; and bring the fattened calf, kill it,
and let us eat and celebrate; for this son
of mine was dead and has come to life
again; he was lost and has been found.'
And they began to celebrate.

Jesus speaks about the father waiting for his son and searching the distant road. In fact, the father notices his son while he is still a long way off. The son is still in his sin, yet he made the decision to go back home.

This parable shows that we should never give up, no matter how far away we seem to be. God is patient and gracious with all of us. He is willing to welcome each of us home into His loving and forgiving arms. He doesn't even dwell on our past life of sin. It's very hard for a lot of people to fully grasp how He can forgive without making us feel worse, including me. If God does that with us, how can we not do that with each other?

When our loved ones finally come to their senses and realize they can't live any longer without God in their lives, who are we to continue to bring up their past? In this story, the son tells his father, "I am no longer worthy to be called your son." The father doesn't even acknowledge what the son said. Rather, he orders the servants to dress his son with the best clothes and orders a feast and celebration to be thrown in his honor. His son was now back home.

Hebrews 8:12 (NASB—For I will be merciful to their iniquities, and I will remember their sins no more.

How to Fight for Your Marriage

My sister, Amy had been praying for my husband Brian and I for a long time. She was one of the few who continued to pray for him when all others had stopped. She knew the Lord's desire was for us to be together.

Instead of praying according to the situation, she prayed according to what the Lord spoke to her. She called me one day and told me what the Lord had spoken to her during prayer. She said the Lord spoke to her about a lion's roar.

When a lion gets close to the ground, its roar can be heard for miles because the vibrations of the roar can travel a considerable distance. It warns others to stay away and to back off from their territory.

The Lord was telling me that I needed to go into prayer and become like a lion. I need to send out a message to the enemy that he was not going to win this battle. In the Bible, the enemy is referred to many times as a lion, but God's people are also referred to as lions.

I discovered some of the reason's lions roar. One of the reasons was to intimidate rivals during aggressive interactions. When the enemy is coming against your family and coming against your marriage, that is an aggressive interaction. We, as women, need to rise up and take our families back.

God's word tells us to be sober (serious) and vigilant (alert and watchful) because the enemy does walk about as a roaring lion seeking whom he may devour. His intention is to destroy us.

The enemy wants us to look at him and listen to his lies. He roars to make us afraid. Notice in this verse it says that our enemy is as a roaring lion. In other words, he parades around as a lion, but he is not the real lion. Jesus is the Lion of the tribe of Judah and the victory belongs to him.

1 Peter 5:8 (NASB)—Be of sober spirit, be on the alert. Your adversary, the devil, prowls around like a roaring lion, seeking someone to devour.

So, how do you "fight" for your marriage if your opponent is one that can't be seen? It's not like you can just punch the devil in the face and he will run away with his tail tucked between his legs. There is an invisible world and there is an invisible war. We call it spiritual warfare. If it takes place in the spiritual/unseen realm, then how do we fight? In the Bible spiritual warfare is described in this way…

2 Corinthians 10:3–6 (NASB)— "For though we walk in the flesh, we do not war according to the flesh, for the weapons of our warfare are not of the flesh, but divinely powerful for the destruction of fortresses. We are destroying speculations and every lofty thing raised up against the knowledge of God, and we are taking every thought captive to the obedience of Christ, and we are ready to punish all disobedience, whenever your obedience is complete.

We can't battle Satan in the flesh because we are not equal rivals. We need the Holy Spirit to back up our authority. Truthfully, we have all authority in Jesus to root out, pull down, and destroy.

We can't drive demons into obedience when we are disobeying the word of God in any area. Before you engage in spiritual warfare, do a heart check, ask God to forgive you and ask for His guidance. He is faithful to help us if we ask him.

Fighting for my marriage was something I found very difficult to do. I found myself wanting to fight one day and wanting to give up the next. It's very difficult when your opponent looks very much like your spouse.

Even though I would read the Bible about not battling with flesh and blood, it was hard for me because I was staring down flesh and blood. My flesh and blood husband seemed to be the one causing all this hurt and pain in my and my children's life. I didn't understand what 2 Corinthians 10:3–6 meant at all.

Therefore, by not comprehending it, I didn't know how to use it. The Bible is full of scriptures that we can use and apply in our life, but if we do not grasp their meanings, they're not very useful.

I yearned to know so I began searching out different scriptures. What does it mean to war in the spirit? How does one do that? What does it look like? And what are the benefits?

In all honesty, a lot of times after praying for Brian, I would leave still feeling angry with him. Sometimes I would get a message on my phone from him shortly after I've prayed and immediately get into an anger fit all over again.

It seemed like a losing battle I had to fight day after day. I needed to know: what are my weapons for fighting this battle that I am in? And how do I use them?

I'm guessing there are a lot more people like me. People that want to fight for their spouse, fight for their marriage, but just not sure how, when, or why. What if you found out someone had planned to take you out, ruin your life, ruin your marriage, ruin your children, split your church, have you feeling overwhelmed, deceived, and believing lies?

I'm sure you would be like me and put a stop to that right away. Well that is exactly what the enemy wants to do to each one of us. That is why the Lord gives us the tools to combat the enemy when he comes after us, because it is not a matter of if. It's a matter of when.

1. What does it mean to war in the spirit?

Many do not believe there is a spiritual realm. Just because you do not believe it, does not mean it does not exist. This is the realm where angels and demons exist.

There are many who have seen an angel or encountered a demon. When this happened, they had a glimpse into the spiritual realm. Many people do not want to deal with a world they cannot see because quite frankly it's a little hard to believe.

It's important to believe in the spiritual realm. We think that covering our eyes means what we do not see is not actually there. Wrong! The spiritual realm is there, and there is a battle going on whether we choose to believe it or not.

The best thing to do is get educated on this subject, which is half the fight. If we choose not to believe in the spiritual realm, we will only find ourselves confused and frustrated by what is going on in our lives.

The first step when you war in the spirit is to believe that the spirit realm exists. It's our part to believe. If you struggle with this area, ask the Lord to help you believe. He will. I struggled in this area as well. There are a lot of good books out now just on this subject.

2.   How does one war in the Spirit?

Spiritual warfare is a war between the forces of God and the forces of the devil. How do we warfare for those people in our family? We pray.

We start on our knees before God. We cannot physically go grab a sword and start cutting demons to pieces; however, we can call out to the God of all the heavens and ask him to go into battle for us and push back the forces of darkness.

If you can just close your eyes for a moment and imagine as you pray that God is sending out instructions to His angels to combat the demons that are at work. It is powerful if you think about it. One simple act of prayer on our part can do so much. That is why the enemy likes to keep us from praying. How often is it that we find anything and everything to do but pray?

When we decide to stop everything and pray to God, the phone starts ringing, and the kids start fighting. There is interruption after interruption. However, we can sit on the couch, searching Facebook for an hour and encounter zero interruptions? It's because the enemy knows what he's doing.

He also knows that we are powerful in prayer. If he can keep us from a place of prayer, then he has won. That is why it is so very important to find time to pray. Tell the kids what you are doing and close the door, and if you must lock the door, do it.

Prayer is very important. It is the key to everything. How do you expect your situation to change when you don't even pray about? I challenge you, if you haven't prayed about your current situation, make a point to start today and watch what the Lord does.

3.   **What are my weapons?**

(1). Our first weapon is the name of Jesus. The devil hates that name. Just one mention of His name and chains begin to break. When you feel a spiritual attack in your life, use the name of Jesus. There is just something about the Name.

Proverbs 18:10 (NASB)—The name of the Lord is a strong tower; the righteous runs into it and is safe.

(2). The second weapon is the blood of Jesus. His blood is a covering. Even while Brian was out running around, I would pray the blood of Jesus around him.

You can place a blood covering over your family and the enemy cannot cross the blood line. When Jesus shed His blood, he conquered sin. When I pray, I plead the blood of Jesus over my life, my family, and my future.

Imagine when you pray the blood of Jesus over your spouse a truckload of blood being poured over him. It would be impossible to see through to the person inside. That is what happens when we pray the blood of Jesus over someone. They are hidden behind the blood!

> (3). The third weapon is the Word of God. In Ephesians 6:17 the sword of the Spirit is the Word of God or the Bible. It is a powerful weapon that few people realize we can use. I did not realize just how powerful it is until I started to research it out.

The Bible is powerful because the enemy cannot make the Word fail. Truth cannot fail. When you claim the promises of God in your life they become active. They become alive!

> *Hebrews 4:12 (NASB)—For the word of God is living and active and sharper than any two-edged sword and piercing as far as the division of soul and spirit, of both joints and marrow, and able to judge the thoughts and intentions of the heart.*

When you pray the scriptures against the enemy, you will begin to see change. I want to encourage you to look up scriptures and promises in the Bible that pertain to your situation. For me, I looked up scriptures about my household.

> *Acts 16:31 (NASB)—They said, "Believe in the Lord Jesus, and you will be saved, you and your household."*

(4). The fourth weapon is prayer. Prayer is our communication with God. We bring our requests and decrees before Him on behalf of our loved ones and us. Prayer is so important in our walk with the Lord.

How can you say you know someone you never talk to? You need to stay prayed up. If you let your guard down, you become vulnerable to the enemy. Daily prayer is letting God know He is really in control of our lives. God invites us to bring our concerns, our problems, and trials to Him and to share with Him our joy and victories. And He communicates back to us

Jeremiah 33:3 (NASB)—Call to Me and I will answer you, and I will tell you great and mighty things, which you do not know.

(5). The fifth weapon is the Holy Spirit. Many people do not realize that the Holy Spirit is the active force of God in our lives to help us. We need the power of the Holy Spirit working in us and through us. He is constantly moving on our behalf.

He is our friend and is for us and not against us. He knows us better than we know ourselves. He is the kind of friend I would want fighting on my behalf. When you pray, declare those things out into the spiritual realm. In other words, say them out loud. The devil cannot read your thoughts, so pray the scriptures out loud and watch how fast he runs.

4. How do I use my weapons?

> *Ephesians 6:13–18 (NASB)—Therefore, take up the full armor of God, so that you will be able to resist in the evil day, and having done everything, to stand firm Stand firm therefore, having girded your loins with truth, and having put on the breastplate of righteousness, and having shod your feet with the preparation of the gospel of peace; in addition to all, taking up the shield of faith with which you will be able to extinguish all the flaming arrows of the evil one. And take the helmet of salvation, and the sword of the Spirit, which is the word of God. With all prayer and petition pray at all times in the Spirit, and with this in view, be on the alert with perseverance and petition for all the saints.*

In battle we need to stand firm. The enemy will try over and over to knock us down and he may succeed but stand back up.

> *Proverbs 24: 16 (NASB)—For a righteous man falls seven times and rises again.*

Even if the enemy was successful in knocking us down, he can't keep us down. Stand back up and show him you are not easily taken out. He only wins if we stay down.

I want to encourage you today. Even if you were knocked down and it has been a while since you have stood again, today is a new day, find your legs and stand back up.

The enemy has a whole arsenal of things he will use to make sure we go down and keeps us down. Ultimately the choice to stay down is ours. He knocked me down over and over. Sometimes I got back up quickly, other times I laid down for a while, but I never stayed down. The victory is when you stand again.

The armor of God gives us the power to stand against the deception of the enemy. The enemy wants to deceive us. The mind is a spiritual battlefield, and without the helmet of salvation it is impossible to have a victorious life in Christ.

When we wear the helmet of salvation, it empowers us to continually renew our minds. The breastplate of righteousness covers the chest. This part of the armor is very important because it covers the heart, the seat of our emotions. We must be careful of the seeds we allow to be planted in our hearts.

> ***Psalms 51:10 (NASB)—Create in
> me a clean heart, O God, and renew a
> steadfast spirit within me.***

The Bible says to gird your loins with truth. It is only the truth that can keep even a believer sexually pure. God gives us a way of escape every time the enemy lays a snare to trap us. If you are a man or woman who has been bound by sexual impurity, repent and go the other way. Fill yourself with God's truth and walk out of the enemy's stronghold.

It is important that our feet are shod with the gospel of peace. We may make some mistakes, but God ultimately delivers us into victory if we come to Him. When we walk in the gospel of peace, it prepares a path for our way to be prosperous, and we are at one with the will of God for our lives.

The sword of the spirit is an offensive and defensive weapon. It can be used to attack and to protect. The sword of the spirit is the word of God. When we pray the word, it comes out of our mouth like a double-edged sword and attacks the enemy.

In Ephesians 6:16 it talks about the shield of faith being used to stop the fiery darts of the enemy. This is a very important part of our defense. A shield covers and protects. Without this weapon, we are left exposed to the enemy and will ultimately be injured.

Praying in the Spirit is the part of the armor that we use offensively, but it becomes a defense to those for which we are praying or standing in the gap for. As we pray in the Spirit, our enemies will be shut down.

We need to put on the full armor of God daily. Leaving even one piece off will expose us to the enemy. God has given us each piece and no part works alone. The whole armor of God helps us to ward off the attacks of the enemy.

Beauty from Ashes

I'm sure there are many who have lived or are currently living through a story like mine, and they did not have the same outcome or are currently facing divorce. I sit here and wonder: why did my marriage make it and so many do not?

After everything we have gone through, why didn't my marriage end up on the long and seemingly never-ending wall of divorce? Everything that happened certainly made my marriage a good candidate for divorce. Does this mean my marriage is more important than the ones that did not make it? Certainly not!

The Bible has a high view of marriage. Its original design is to be a lifetime plan, not a convenience that can be thrown away. A love between a husband and a wife is a small glimmer of the deeper love between God and us. God established marriage as a covenant, not a contract

A covenant is more binding than a contract. We persevered when the entire situation said the marriage covenant was over. There is hope for anyone who desires his or her marriage to be healed. And there is hope that there is a God who does desire good for us. He can turn our messes into something beautiful. We are never too far gone that God can't reach down and turn our situations around. If He did that for us, He will do that for anyone.

> *Acts 10:34 (NASB)—Opening his mouth, Peter said: "I most certainly understand now that God is not one to show partiality"*

What He did for my marriage, He can and will do for anyone. We only must believe.

> *Mark 11:23 (NASB)— "Truly I say to you, whoever says to this mountain, 'Be taken up and cast into the sea,' and does not doubt in his heart, but believes that what he says is going to happen, it will be granted him."*

Doubt was something I had to give to God. I wanted to believe things had changed, but I had seen the opposite so many times. Overcoming doubt was where I had to rely heavily on God. Honestly, He knows this is a difficult task and He will help you.

He wants to help you. We don't have to walk through this life alone. He wants us to lean on Him and to come to him with our fears, our broken hearts, and our disappointments. He promises to help us.

*Psalm 46:1(NASB)—God is our
refuge and strength, a very present help
in trouble.*

I found this to be very true in my own life. It never failed when I was hurt and wanting to quit, he would send someone my way to encourage me. When I wanted to end it all, He sent supernatural intervention to stop it. There was encouragement all around me. Sometimes I just couldn't see it. It was hard to see two feet in front of me at times.

Once the fog cleared, I could see where God's hand was all along. I am a living testimony that He truly never does leave us, and He truly never will forsake us. Although we may feel forsaken, God will always be in our corner fighting for us. We may have been the one who stepped away from Him, yet He will never leave us. Now that is love!

*John 3:16 (NASB)—"For God so
loved the world, that He gave His only
begotten Son, that whoever believes in
Him shall not perish, but have eternal
life."*

John 3:16 is a verse we have all probably heard many times. If we really read it, it is quite astonishing. Frankly I couldn't give my own as a sacrifice for my own family much less someone I didn't even know.

God loves us with no end and no conditions. He loves us regardless of our sin and regardless of all the mess we bring to the table. In fact, He helps us clean up our mess, the mess He didn't even create. Then He helps us walk the road to a more fulfilling life, which has Jesus Christ at the center of it.

Brian and I learned the hard way. Although I had all that church upbringing, I still had to apply what I learned to my own life. I couldn't rely on my parents to do it for me. I had to choose to add Jesus Christ to my life on my own.

The truth is that a life without God is harder, less fulfilling, and constantly lacking. A life with God is not always easier, but we know the One who knows our tomorrow, and can help us and lead us through all of life's troubles.

Without God we are walking around blindly, just hoping we are getting it right. I've gone that route too and hoping without God goes about as far as the word itself. Hope with God empowers us.

God is our Creator, and we are designed by His own purpose for Him. I'm sure you've heard the saying, "There is a God shape hope in all of us." And that is exactly true. There is a place inside of us that longs for our Creator and only He can fill it.

Without Him, we look for things to fill that void. Nothing will fill it to its fullness like God. Anything we do fill it will hold our happiness for a little bit. It always fades leaving us looking and searching for something or someone to fill that void again. God is the only one who can fill that void and make you feel complete and whole.

People are always searching for something to make them feel complete. The devil will put all these things in front of us, trying to make us think that need it. He tries to keep you so distracted with searching out things, the newest cell phone, the best job, the bigger house, the nicest car, the best friends and the list can go on and on.

Those things are not bad, but when the things become more important than God, then it becomes bad. The devil is always trying to distract, overwhelm, distort, downplay, maneuver, and lie. He will use anyone or anything to keep you away from God. The only way you can discern the difference between what is from God and what is not, is to know him.

Brian and I made a lot of wrong choices in our lives before we started making the right ones. That seems to be the case with a lot of people. I am so thankful for a God who looks past our mistakes, forgives them, and loves us anyway.

Looking back over my life and everything that has happened, I can honestly say that God has made my marriage better than it was before. How crazy is it to think that a marriage can become better through all the mess, but it can! He makes all things new. He takes the mess and turns it into something breathtaking.

It all started when we both surrendered individually to God. He took the wasteland of our lives and made it a garden that now beautiful things grow in. This book was not designed to give the enemy one ounce of glory, but to point a huge spot light on what God did for us. I owe Him everything. I owe Him my family. If I live one hundred life times, I could never repay Him for what He has done for me. It is a sweet victory.

I had to give up the control I thought I had over my husband and give him completely over to God. Once I stepped out of the way, God could work. But the thing is, while God was working on Brian, He started pointing out things in me that was not pleasing to Him. It's easy to find other people's shortcomings, but we look at ourselves as the model of what everyone else should be and do. It's harder to see the plank in our own eye.

Matthew 7:3–5 (NASB)—"Why
do you look at the speck that is in your
brother's eye, but do not notice the log

that is in your own eye? Or how can you say to your brother, 'Let me take the speck out of your eye,' and behold, the log is in your own eye? You hypocrite first take the log out of your own eye, and then you will see clearly to take the speck out of your brother's eye."

I was so focused on Brian's sin, because it was highly visible. Anyone could point a finger and point out his sin. My sin was one that was hidden and couldn't be easily pointed out. My sin was something that had to do with my heart. Others didn't easily detect it; however, it was not hidden from God.

I had allowed a lot of things to enter my heart and became a very angry person. I felt victimized and entitled to it. I had allowed jealousy to become my identity. I didn't trust women. It considered them to be my competition for keeping Brian as my husband, and they were a potential source of pain.

I was anxious almost all the time, which also made my children anxious, and it played out in other avenues of my life. I was sick most of the time because of all the anxiety. I was filled with fear and every decision I made was based out of fear.

I didn't trust people. I expected them to hurt me, so I kept a wall built up high that made it impossible for anyone to know me or even help me. The person I had become pushed people away instead of drawing them close.

I was prickly yet desperate for friendship. I had turned into my own worst enemy. I was angry, bitter, resentful, fearful, and anxious. These things had become my identity and I functioned out of them mostly.

God started pointing things out to me that I needed to let go of. It was difficult because they had become my identity. If I gave up being a victim, then who was I?

I was afraid that letting go of being a victim was sending Brian the message that what he's done was all right with me. What a lie from the enemy! Satan wanted the victim mentality to stay my identity because if I let it, I would never truly forgive. Therefore, I would continually stay a slave to never forgiving people. I would be a prisoner, not anyone else.

I used to think that I must have done something bad in my life and I was deserving of all this bad stuff that was coming against me. I even wondered if God was mad at me or even hated me. I didn't understand how so much wrong could happen to one person.

The enemy likes to lie and make us think it's all God's fault. The Bible clearly states that God does not treat us how we deserve, but He loves us despite all our sin.

Psalm 103:10 (NASB)—He has not dealt with us according to our sins, nor rewarded us according to our iniquities.

No matter what we have done He does not treat us the way our sin deserves but He loves us and accepts us. There is nothing we can do that will push our loving heavenly Father away from us. Nothing!

I know it's hard to comprehend, especially if we've walked down a difficult road, but listen to me now—There is nothing we have done that disqualifies us. There is nowhere we have gone that will push Him away.

He wants us to come to Him now with all of our baggage. He wants it all. He is not repulsed or disgusted. If we could see His eyes towards us right now, we would see eyes burning with love for us. No judgment just love.

> *Psalm 103:11–12 (NASB)—For as high as the heavens are above and the earth, so great is his loving kindness toward those who fear Him. As far as the east is from the west, so far has He removed our transgressions from us.*

He removes our sins and remembers them no more!

> *Hebrews 8:12 (NASB)—"For I will be merciful to their iniquities, and I will remember their sins no more."*

Do you desperately want your sins forgiven and not to be remembered again? I encourage you to ask God to forgive you for them. He is the only one who can pardon your sins and wipe them from His memory. He'll give you a fresh start and put you back on the right road again.

I once heard someone say that when we walk away from God and get off the road leading to our destiny, we think we will have to go right back to the starting place to get back on the right path. Serving God is a lot like a GPS in a car. When you take a wrong turn, the GPS does not lead you back to your starting location, it recalculates your position to get you back on the right path to your destination. That's how it is with God.

Many times, in our lives we take a wrong turn and get out of the will of God. When we realize what we have done and repent for the wrong direction, God recalibrates our destiny from where we are to get us back on the right path.

All those things we did along the way, He can use to help us. Those terrible things we've have gone through in our lives were not God's plan for us. He can heal us and make us into something beautiful.

In turn, we can help others with what we have gone through. That is the ultimate revenge against the enemy. It's using what he meant for our destruction and allowing God to use it for His glory.

This is my reason for writing this book. I want to bring glory to God for what He did for my marriage. I want to let the world know that God can restore. There is no device of the enemy that God cannot turn around and use for our good.

> ***Romans 8:28 (NASB)—And we know that God causes all things to work together for good to those who love God, to those who are called according to His purpose.***

Since Brian and I have reconciled back to each other and back to God, we have been ministering at different places here and there sharing our testimony of what God did for our marriage. Our story is a story of hope through even the darkest of situations. There is no mountain too high, no valley too low, and no ocean too wide that God cannot reach down and bring forth life out of it.

I pray that our story has encouraged you to keep fighting the good fight. The only time we lose the battle is when we lay our weapons down. If you have laid your weapons down, I encourage you to repent, and pick those weapons back up. Get back in the fight for your family. If there is any battle worth fighting, it is the battle for those we love.

If you are like Brian and I, and have stepped away from God, or maybe you have never made the commitment to serve Him and would like to make that change today, I invite you to say this prayer with me and mean it with all your heart!

Romans 10:9 (NASB)—If you confess with your mouth Jesus as Lord and believe in your heart that God raised Him from the dead, you will be saved.

Dear Heavenly Father,

I know I have broken your laws and my sins have separated me from you. I am truly sorry and now I want to turn away from my past sinful life toward You. Please forgive me and help me avoid sinning again. I believe that Your son, Jesus Christ died for my sins, was resurrected from the dead, is alive, and hears my prayers. I invite You, Jesus, to become the Lord of my life, to rule and reign in my heart from this day forward.

Please send Your Holy Spirit to help me obey You, and to do Your will for the rest of my life. In Jesus name I pray, Amen!

If you said this prayer, I encourage you to tell someone. Find a church where you can learn more about the God I speak of in this book. The God who changed my life and my husband's life can do the same for yours.

Our Weapons for the Fight—Word of God

During all the difficult times in my marriage, I was being lied to quite a bit. Not only did my husband lie, but also the devil. He was wreaking havoc in my thoughts and getting me to buy into all these lies about my husband, about my children, about my family and even about my future and myself.

It was a steady barrage of lies being thrown into my mind daily. I would go to the hospital to work a twelve-hour shift, and the devil would start tormenting me with all these thoughts about my husband. What was he doing right then? Who was he with? Where was he going? The thoughts alone would drive me crazy. It was a battle daily in my mind, and it was one I seemed to lose quite often.

Since the Bible tells me the devil is the father of lies and there is no truth in him, I decided to list some scripture from the Bible that helped me in my most difficult times. They reminded me of God's promises and plans for me and helped me hang on for one more day.

->> Fear <<-

Isaiah 41:10 (NASB)—So do not fear, for I am with you; do not be dismayed for I am your God. I will strengthen you and help you; I will uphold you with my righteous right hand.

Psalm 56:3 (NASB)—When I am afraid, I will put my trust in you.

Philippians 4:6–7 (NASB)—Be anxious for nothing, but in everything by prayer and supplication with thanksgiving let our requests be made known to God. And the peace of God, which surpasses all comprehension, will guard your hearts and minds in Christ Jesus.

John 14:27 (NASB)—Peace I leave with you; My peace I give you; not as the world gives do I give to you. Do not let your heart be troubled, nor let it be fearful.

2 Timothy 1:7 (NASB)—For God has not given us a spirit of timidity, but of power and love and discipline.

1 John 4:18 (NASB)—There is no fear in love; but perfect love casts out fear, because fear involves punishment, and the one who fears is not perfected in love.

Psalm 94:19 (NASB)—When my anxious thoughts multiply within me, your consolations delight my soul.

Isaiah 43:1 (NASB)—But now, thus says the Lord, your Creator, O Jacob, and He who formed you, O Israel, "Do not fear, for I have redeemed you; I have called you by name; you are Mine!"

Proverbs 12:25 (NASB)—Anxiety in a man's heart weighs it down, but a good word makes it glad.

Psalm 23:4 (NASB)—Even though I walk through the valley of the shadow of death, I fear no evil, for You are with me; Your rod and Your staff, they comfort me.

Joshua 1:9 (NASB)—Have I not commanded you? Be strong and courageous! Do not tremble or be dismayed, for the Lord your God is with you wherever you go."

Matthew 6:34 (NASB)—"So do not worry about tomorrow, for tomorrow will care for itself. Each day has enough trouble of its own.

1 Peter 5:6–7 (NASB)—Therefore humble yourselves under the mighty hand of God, that He may exalt you at the proper time, casting all your anxiety on Him, because He cares for you.

Isaiah 35:4 (NASB)—Say to those with anxious heart, "Take courage, fear not. Behold your God will come with vengeance; the recompense of God will come, but he will save you."

Luke 12:22–26 (NASB)—And He said to His disciples, "For this reason I say to you, do not worry about your life, as to what you will eat; nor for your body, as to what you will put on. For life is more than food, and the body more than clothing. Consider the ravens, for they neither sow nor reap; they have no storeroom nor barn, and yet God feeds them; how much more valuable you are than the birds! And which of you by worrying can add a single hour to his life's span? If then you cannot do even a very little thing, why do you worry about other matters?

Psalm 27:1 (NASB)—The Lord is my light and my salvation—whom shall I fear? The Lord is the stronghold of my life—of whom shall I be afraid?

Psalm 55:22 (NASB)—Cast your cares on the Lord and he will sustain you; he will never let the righteous fall.

Mark 6:50 (NASB)—Immediately he spoke to them and said, "Take courage! It is I, don't be afraid."

Deuteronomy 31:6 (NASB)—Be strong and courageous. Do not be afraid or terrified because of them, for the Lord your God goes with you; he will never leave you nor forsake you.

Isaiah 41:13–14 (NASB)—For I am the Lord, your God, who takes hold of your right hand and says to you, "Do not fear; I will help you. Do not be afraid, for I myself will help you," declares the Lord, your Redeemer, the Holy One of Israel.

Psalm 46:1 (NASB)—God is our refuge and strength, an ever-present help in trouble.

Psalm 118:6–7 (NASB)—The Lord is with me; I will not be afraid. What can man do to me? The Lord is with me; he is my helper.

Proverbs 29:25 (NASB)—Fear of man will prove to be a snare, but whoever trusts in the Lord is kept safe.

Psalm 34:7 (NASB)—The Angel of the Lord encamps around those who fear him, and he delivers them.

1 Peter 3:14 (NASB)—But even if you suffer for doing what is right, God will reward you for it. So, don't worry or be afraid of their threats.

Psalm 34:4 (NASB)—I prayed to the Lord, and he answered me. He freed me from all my fears.

Deuteronomy 3:22 (NASB)—Do not be afraid of them; the Lord your God Himself will fight for you.

Revelation 1:17 (NASB)—Then He placed His right hand on me and said: "Do not be afraid. I am the first and the Last."

Mark 5:36 (NASB)—Jesus told him, "Don't be afraid, just believe."

Romans 8:38–39 (NASB)—And I am convinced that nothing can ever separate us from God's love. Neither death nor life, neither angels nor demons, neither our fears for today nor our worries about tomorrow—not even the powers of hell can separate us from God's love.

Psalms 91:1–16 (NASB)—He who dwells in the shelter of the Most High will rest in the shadow of the Almighty. I will say of the Lord, "He is my refuge and my fortress, my God, in whom I trust."… He will cover you with his feathers and under his wings you will find refuge; his faithfulness will be your shield and rampart. You will not fear the terror of night, nor the arrow that flies by day, nor the pestilence that stalks in the darkness, nor the plague that destroys at midday. A thousand may fall at your side, ten thousand at your right hand, but it will not come near you. For he will command his angels concerning you, to guard you in all your ways…"Because he loves me," says the Lord, "I will rescue him; I will protect him, for he acknowledges my name. He will call upon me, and I will answer him; I will be with him in trouble, I will deliver him and honor him…"

->> **Anger** <<-

Ephesians 4:26–31 (NASB)—Be angry, and yet do not sin; do not let the sun go down on your anger, and do not give the devil an opportunity. He who steals must steal no longer; but rather he must labor, performing with his own hands what is good, so that he will have something to share with one who has need. Let no unwholesome word proceed from your mouth, but only such a word as is good for edification according to the need of the moment, so that it will give grace to those who hear. Do not grieve the Holy Spirit of God, by whom you were sealed for the day of redemption. Let all bitterness and wrath and anger and clamor and slander be put away from you, along with malice.

James 1:19–20 (NASB)—This you know, my beloved brethren. But everyone must be quick to hear, slow to speak and slow to anger; for the anger of man does not achieve the righteousness of God.

Proverbs 29:11 (NASB)—A fool always loses his temper, but a wise man holds it back.

Proverbs 19:11 (NASB)—A man's discretion makes him slow to anger, and it is his glory to overlook a transgression.

Ecclesiastes 7:9 (NASB)—Do not be eager in your heart to be angry, for anger resides in the bosom of fools.

Proverbs 15:1 (NASB)—A gentle answer turns away wrath, but a harsh word stirs up anger.

Proverbs 15:18 (NASB)—A hot-tempered man stirs up strife, but the slow to anger calms a dispute.

Colossians 3:8 (NASB)—But now you also, put them all aside: anger, wrath, malice, slander and abusive speech from your mouth.

James 4:1–2 (NASB)—What is the source of quarrels and conflicts among you? Is not the source your pleasures that wage war in your members? You lust and do not have; so you commit murder. You are envious and cannot obtain; so you fight and quarrel. You do not have because you do not ask.

Proverbs 16: 32 (NASB)—He who is slow to anger is better than the mighty, and he who rules his spirit, than he who captures a city.

Proverbs 22:24 (NASB)—Do not associate with a man given to anger; or go with a hot-tempered man.

Matthew 5:22 (NASB)—But I say to you everyone who is angry with his brother shall be guilty before the court; and whoever says to his brother, 'You good-for-nothing,' shall be guilty before the supreme court; and whoever says, 'You fool,' shall be guilty enough to go into the fiery hell.

Psalm 37:8–9 (NASB)—Cease from anger and forsake wrath; do not fret; it leads only to evildoing. For evildoers will be cut off, but those who wait for the lord, they will inherit the land.

Proverbs 14:29 (NASB)—He who is slow to anger has great understanding, but he who is quick-tempered exalts the folly.

->> Forgiveness <<-

Matthew 6:14–15 (NASB)—For if you forgive others for their transgressions, your heavenly Father will also forgive you. But if you do not forgive others, then your Father will not forgive your transgressions.

1 John 1:9 (NASB)—If we confess our sins, He is faithful and righteous to forgive us our sins and to cleanse us from all unrighteousness.

Acts 3:19 (NASB)—Therefore repent and return, so that your sins may be wiped away, in order that times of refreshing may come from the presence of the Lord.

Isaiah 1:18 (NASB)—"Come now, and let us reason together," says the Lord, "Though your sins are as scarlet, they will be white as snow; though they are red like crimson, they will be like wool."

2 Corinthians 5:17 (NASB)—Therefore if anyone is in Christ, he is a new creature; the old things passed away; behold, new things have come.

Ephesians 1:7 (NASB)—In Him we have redemption through His blood, the forgiveness of our trespasses, according to the riches of His grace.

Hebrews 10:17 (NASB)—"And their sins and their lawless deeds I will remember no more."

Daniel 9:9 (NASB)—To the Lord our God belong compassion and forgiveness, for we have rebelled against Him.

Colossians 1:13–14 (NASB)—For He rescued from the domain of darkness and transferred us to the kingdom of His beloved Son, in whom we have redemption, the forgiveness of sins.

Psalm 103:12 (NASB)—As far as the east is from the west, so far has He removed our transgressions from us.

Micah 7:18–19 (NASB)—Who is a God like You, who pardons iniquity and passes over the rebellious act of the remnant of His possession? He does not retain His anger forever, because He delights in unchanging love. He will again have compassion on us; He will tread our iniquities under foot. Yes, You will cast all their sins into the depths of the sea.

Matthew 6:9–15 (NASB)—"Pray, then this way: 'Our Father who is in heaven, hallowed by Your name. Your kingdom comes. Your will be done, on earth as it is in heaven. Give us this day our daily bread. And forgive us our debts, as we also have forgiven our debtors. And do not lead us into temptation but deliver us from evil. For yours is the kingdom and the power and the glory forever. Amen.'

Mark 11:25 (NASB)—Whenever you stand praying, forgive, if you have anything against anyone, so that your Father who is in heaven will also forgive you your transgressions.

Matthew 26:28 (NASB)—For this is My blood of the covenant, which is poured out for many for forgiveness of sins.

->> Hope <<-

Jeremiah 29:11 (NASB)—For I know the plans that I have for you,' declares the Lord, 'plans for welfare and not for calamity to give you a future and a hope.

Psalm 42:11 (NASB)—Why are you in despair, O my soul" And why have you become disturbed within me? Hope in God, for I shall yet praise Him, the help of my countenance and my God.

Isaiah 40:31 (NASB)—Yet those who wait for the Lord will gain new strength; they will mount up with wings like eagles, they will run and not get tired, they will walk and not become weary.

Psalm 121:7–8 (NASB)—The Lord will protect you from all evil; He will keep your soul. The Lord will guard your going out and your coming in from this time forth and forever.

Romans 15:13 (NASB)—Now may the God of hope fill you with all joy and peace in believing, so that you will abound in hope by the power of the Holy Spirit.

Hebrews 11:1 (NASB)—Now faith is the assurance of things hoped for, the conviction of things not seen.

Matthew 11:28 (NASB)—"Come to Me, all who are weary and heavy-laden, and I will give you rest."

1 Corinthians 13:13 (NASB)—But now faith, hope, love, abide these three; but the greatest of these is love.

Psalm 119:114 (NASB)—You are my hiding place and my shield; I wait for Your word.

Psalm 31:24 (NASB)—Be strong and let your heart take courage, all you who hope in the Lord.

Hebrews 10:23 (NASB)—Let us hold fast the confession of our hope without wavering, for He who promised is faithful.

Proverbs 13:12 (NASB)—Hope deferred makes the heart sick, but desire fulfilled is a tree of life.

Romans 8:25 (NASB)—But if we hope for what we do not see, with perseverance we wait eagerly for it.

Psalm 130:5 (NASB)—I wait for the Lord, my soul does wait, and in His word do I hope.

Isaiah 61:1 (NASB)—The Spirit of the Lord God is upon me, because the Lord has anointed me to bring good news to the afflicted; He has sent me to bind up the brokenhearted, to proclaim liberty to captives and freedom to prisoners.

1 Peter 3:15 (NASB)—But sanctify Christ as Lord in your hearts, always being ready to make a defense to everyone who asks you to give an account for the hope that is in you, yet with gentleness and reverence.

Romans 5:3–4 (NASB)—And not only this, but we also exult in our tribulations, knowing that tribulation brings about perseverance; and perseverance, proven character; and proven character, hope.

Psalm 33:22 (NASB)—Let your lovingkindness, O Lord, be upon us, according as we have hoped in You.

1 Peter 1:3 (NASB)—Blessed be the God and Father of our Lord Jesus Christ, who according to His great mercy has caused us to be born again to a living hope through the resurrection of Jesus Christ from the dead.

Ephesians 4:4 (NASB)—There is one body and one Spirit, just as you also were called in one hope of your calling.

Romans 5:5 (NASB)—And hope does not disappoint, because the love of God has been poured out within our hearts through the Holy Spirit who was given to us.

Micah 7:7 (NASB)—But as for me, I will watch expectantly for the Lord; I will wait for the God of my salvation. My God will hear me.

Psalm 25:5 (NASB)—Lead me in Your truth and teach me, for You are the God of my salvation; for You I wait all day.

Lamentations 3:24 (NASB)—"The Lord is my portion," says my soul, "Therefore I have hope in Him."

->> **Protection** <<-

I Corinthians 10:13 (NASB)—No temptation has overtaken you, but such as is common to man; and God is faithful, who will not allow you to be tempted beyond what you are able, but with the temptation will provide the way of escape also, so that you will be able to endure it.

2 Thessalonians 3:3 (NASB)—But the Lord is faithful, and He will strengthen and protect you from the evil one.

Deuteronomy 31:6 (NASB)—Be strong and courageous, do not be afraid or tremble at them, for the Lord your God is the one who goes with you. He will not fail you or forsake you.

Isaiah 41:10 (NASB)—'Do not fear, for I am with you; do not anxiously look about you, for I am your God. I will strengthen you, surely I will help you, surely I will uphold you with My righteous right hand.'

Proverbs 2:11 (NASB)—Discretion will guard you, understanding will watch over you.

Psalm 5:11 (NASB)—But let all who take refuge in You be glad, let them ever sing for joy; and may You shelter them, that those who love Your name may exult in You.

Psalm 12:5 (NASB)—"Because of the devastation of the afflicted, because of the groaning of the needy, now I will arise," says the Lord; "I will set him in the safety for which he longs."

Psalm 20:1 (NASB)—May the Lord answer you in the day of trouble! May the name of the God of Jacob set you securely on high!

Psalm 34:19 (NASB)—Many are the afflictions of the righteous, but the Lord delivers him out of them all.

Psalm 46:1 (NASB)—God is our refuge and strength, a very present help in trouble.

Psalm 57:1 (NASB)—Be gracious to me, O God, be gracious to me, for my soul takes refuge in You; and in the shadow of Your wings I will take refuge until destruction passes by.

Psalm 59:1 (NASB)—Deliver me from my enemies, O my God; set me securely on high away from those who rise up against me.

Psalm 138:7 (NASB)—Though I walk in the midst of trouble, You will revive me; You will stretch forth your hand against the wrath of my enemies, and Your right hand will save me.

Psalm 140:4 (NASB)—Keep me, O Lord, from the hands of the wicked; preserve me from violent men who have purposed to trip up my feet.

1 Thessalonians 5:23–24 (NASB)—Now may the God of peace Himself sanctify you entirely; and may your spirit and soul and body be preserved complete, without blame at the coming of our Lord Jesus Christ. Faithful is He who calls you, and He also will bring it to pass.

2 Corinthians 4:8–9 (NASB)—We are afflicted in every way, but not crushed; perplexed, but not despairing; persecuted, but not forsaken; struck down, but not destroyed.

2 Samuel 22:3–4 (NASB)—My God, my rock, in whom I take refuge, my shield and the horn of my salvation, my stronghold and my refuge; my Savior, You save me from violence. "I call upon the Lord, who is worthy to be praised, and I am saved from my enemies."

John 10:28–30 (NASB)—And I give eternal life to them, and they will never perish; and no one will snatch them out of My hand. My Father, who has given them to Me, is greater than all; and no one is able to snatch them out of the Father's hand. I and the Father are one."

Psalm 23 (NASB)—The Lord is my shepherd, I shall not want. He makes me lie down in green pastures; He leads me beside quiet waters. He restores my soul; He guides me in the paths of righteousness for His name's sake. Even though I walk through the valley of the shadow of death, I fear no evil, for You are with me; Your rod and Your staff, they comfort me. You prepare a table before me in the presence of my enemies; You have anointed my head with oil; my cup overflows. Surely goodness and loving kindness will follow me all the days of my life, and I will dwell in the house of the Lord forever.

Psalm 121 (NASB)—I will lift my eyes to the mountains; from where shall my help come? My help comes from the Lord, who made heaven and earth. He will not allow your foot to slip; He who keeps you will not slumber. Behold, He who keeps Israel will neither slumber nor sleep. The Lord is your keeper; the Lord is your shade on your right hand. The sun will not smite you by day, nor the moon at night. The Lord will protect you from all evil; He will keep your soul. The Lord will guard your going out and your coming in from this time forth and forever.

Psalm 91 (NASB)—He who dwells in the shelter of the Most High will abide in the shadow of the Almighty. I will say to the Lord, "My refuge and my fortress, my God, in whom I trust!" For it is He who delivers you from the snare of the trapper and from the deadly pestilence. He will cover you with His pinions, and under His wings you may seek refuge; His faithfulness is a shield and bulwark. You will not be afraid of the terror by night, or the arrow that flies by day; or the pestilence that stalks in darkness, or of the destruction that lays waste at noon. A thousand may fall at your side and ten thousand at your right hand, but it shall not approach you. You will only look on with your eyes and see the recompense of the wicked. For you have made the Lord, my refuge, even the Most High, your dwelling place. No evil will befall you, nor will any plague come near your tent. For He will give His angels charge concerning you, to guard you in all your ways. They will bear you up in their hands, that you do not strike your foot against a stone. You will tread upon the lion and the cobra, the young lion and the serpent you will trample down. "Because he has loved Me, therefore I will deliver him; I will set him securely on high, because he has known My name. He will call upon Me, and I will answer him; I will be with him in trouble; I will rescue him and honor him. With a long life I will satisfy him and let him see My salvation."

->> Depression <<-

Philippians 4:8 (NASB)—Finally, brethren, whatever is true, whatever is honorable, whatever is right, whatever is pure, whatever is lovely, whatever is of good repute, if there is any excellence and if anything, worthy of praise, dwell on these things.

Deuteronomy 31:8 (NASB)—The Lord is the one who goes ahead of you; He will be with you. He will not fail you or forsake you. Do not fear or be dismayed.

Psalm 34:17 (NASB)—The righteous cry and the Lord hears and delivers them out of all their troubles.

Psalm 40:1–3 (NASB)—I waited patiently for the Lord; and He inclined to me and hear my cry. He brought me up out of the pit of destruction, out of the miry clay, and He set my feet upon a rock making my footsteps firm. He put a new song in my mouth, a song of praise to our God; many will see and fear and I'll trust in the Lord.

Psalm 3:3 (NASB)—But You, O Lord, are a shield about me, my glory, and the One who lifts my head.

Psalm 32:10 (NASB)—Many are the sorrows of the wicked, but He who trusts in the Lord, loving kindness shall surround him.

1 Peter 5:6–7 (NASB)—Therefore humble yourselves under the mighty hand of God, that He may exalt you at the proper time, casting all your anxiety on Him, because He cares for you.

John 16:33 (NASB)—"These things I have spoken to you, so that in Me you may have peace. In the world you have tribulation but take courage; I have overcome the world."

Romans 8:38–39 (NASB)—For I am convinced that neither death, nor life, nor angels, nor principalities, nor things present, nor things to come, nor powers, nor height, nor depth, nor any other created thing, will be able to separate us from the love of God, which is in Christ Jesus our Lord.

2 Corinthians 1:3–4 (NASB)—Blessed be the God and Father of our Lord Jesus Christ, the Father of mercies and God of all comfort, who comforts us in all our affliction so that we will be able to comfort those who are in any affliction with the comfort with which we ourselves are comforted by God.

1 Peter 4:12–13 (NASB)—Beloved, do not be surprised at the fiery ordeal among you, which comes upon you for your testing, as though some strange thing were happening to you; but to degree that you share the sufferings of Christ, keep rejoicing, so that also at the revelation of His glory you may rejoice with exultation.

Psalm 37:23–24 (NASB)—The steps of a man are established by the Lord, and He delights in his way. When he falls, he will not be hurled headlong, because the Lord is the One who holds his hand.

->> Faith <<-

Galatians 2:20 (NASB)—I have been crucified with Christ; and it is no longer I who live, but Christ lives in me; and the life which I now live in the flesh I live by faith in the Song of God, who loved me and gave Himself up for me.

James 1:6–7 (NASB)—But he must ask in faith without doubting, for the one who doubts is like the surf of the sea, driven and tossed by the wind. For that man ought not to expect that he will receive anything from the Lord, being a double-minded man, unstable in all his ways.

John 3:16 (NASB)—"For God so loved the world, that He gave His only begotten Son, that whoever believes in Him shall not perish, but have eternal life."

John 3:18 (NASB)—"He who believes in Him is not judged; he who does not believe has been judged already, because he has not believed in the name of the only begotten Son of God.

John 3:36 (NASB)—"He who believes in the Son has eternal life; but he who does not obey the Son will not see life, but the wrath of God abides on him."

->> Worry <<-

Matthew 6:25–34 (NASB)—"For this reason I say to you, do not be worried about your life, as to what you will eat or what you will drink; nor for your body, as to what you will put on. Is not life more than food, and the body more than clothing? Look at the birds of the air, that they do not sow, nor reap nor gather into barns, and yet our heavenly Father feeds them. Are you not worth much more than they? And who of you by being worried can add a single hour to his life? And why are you worried about clothing? Observe how the lilies of the field grow; they do not toil, nor do they spin, yet I say to you that not even Solomon in all his glory clothes himself like one of these. But if God so clothes the grass of the field, which is alive today and tomorrow is thrown into the furnace, will He not much more clothe you? You of little faith! Do not worry then, saying, 'What will we eat'" or 'What will we wear for clothing?' For the Gentiles eagerly seek all these things; for your heavenly Father knows that you need all these things. But seek first His kingdom and His righteousness, and all these things will be added to you. So, do not worry about tomorrow; for tomorrow will care for itself. Each day has enough trouble of its own.

Proverbs 3:5–6 (NASB)—Trust in the Lord with all your heart and do not lean on your own understanding. In all your ways acknowledge Him, and He will make your paths straight.

Philippians 4:6–7 (NASB)—Be anxious for nothing, but in everything by prayer and supplication with thanksgiving let your requests be made known to God. And the peace of God, which surpasses all comprehension, will guard your hearts and your minds in Christ Jesus.

Matthew 11:28–30 (NASB)—'Come to Me, all who are weary and heavy-laden, and I will give you rest. Take My yoke upon you and learn from Me, for I am gentle and humble in heart, and You will find rest for your souls. For My yoke is easy and My burden is light.

John 14:27 (NASB)—Peace I leave with you; My peace I give to you; not as the world gives do I give to you. Do not let your heart be troubled, nor let it be fearful.

Colossians 3:15 (NASB)—Let the peace of Christ rule in your hearts, to which indeed you were called in one body; and be thankful.

Psalm 55:22 (NASB)—Cast your burden upon the Lord and He will sustain you; He will never allow the righteous to be shaken.

Proverbs 12:25 (NASB)—Anxiety in a man's heart weighs it down, but a good word makes it glad.

1 Peter 5:6–8 (NASB)—Therefore humble yourselves under the mighty hand of God, that He may exalt you at the proper time, casting all your anxiety on Him, because He cares for you. Be of sober spirit, be on the alert. Your adversary, the devil, prowls around like a roaring lion, seeking someone to devour.

Psalm 23:4 (NASB)—Even though I walk through the valley of the shadow of death, I fear no evil, for You are with me; Your rod and Your staff, they comfort me.

->> Brokenhearted <<-

Psalm 34:18 (NASB)—The Lord is near to the brokenhearted and saves those who are crushed in spirit.

Psalm 73:26 (NASB)—My flesh and my heart may fail, but God is the strength of my heart and my portion forever.

Isaiah 41:10 (NASB)—Do not fear, for I am with you; do not anxiously look about you, for I am your God. I will strengthen you, surely, I will help you, surely, I will uphold you with My righteous right hand.

John 14:27 (NASB)—"Peace I leave with you; My peace I give to you; not as the world gives do I give to you. Do not let your heart be troubled, nor let it be fearful."

2 Corinthians 12:9 (NASB)—And He said to me, "My grace is sufficient for you, for power is perfected in weakness." Most gladly, therefore, I will rather boast about my weaknesses, so that the power of Christ may dwell in me.

Psalms 55:22 (NASB)—Cast your burden upon the Lord and He will sustain you; He will never allow the righteous to be shaken.

Psalm 147:3 (NASB)—He heals the brokenhearted and binds up their wounds.

Proverbs 3:5–6 (NASB)—Trust in the Lord with all your heart and do not lean on your own understanding. In all your way acknowledge Him, and He will make your paths straight.

1 Peter 4:19 (NASB)—Therefore, those also who suffer according to the will of God shall entrust their souls to a faithful Creator in doing what is right.

Psalm 71:20 (NASB)—You who have shown me many troubles and distresses will revive me again and will bring me up again from the depths of the earth.

Romans 8:18 (NASB)—For I consider that the sufferings of this present time are not worthy to be compared with the glory that is to be revealed to us.

Jeremiah 29:11 (NASB)—'For I know the plans that I have for you,' declares the Lord, 'plans for welfare and not for calamity, to give you a future and a hope.'

2 Corinthians 4:8–10 (NASB)—We are afflicted in every way, but not crushed; perplexed, but not despairing; persecuted, but not forsaken; struck down, but not destroyed; always carrying about in the body the dying of Jesus, so that the life of Jesus also may be manifested in our body.

->> **Frustration** <<-

Galatians 6:9 (NASB)—Let us not lose heart in doing good, for in due time we will reap if we do not grow weary.

Romans 5:1 (NASB)—Therefore, having been justified by faith, we have peace with God through our Lord Jesus Christ.

Joshua 1:9 (NASB)—Have I not commanded you? Be strong and courageous! Do not tremble or be dismayed, for the Lord your God is with you wherever you go.

1 Peter 5:6–7 (NASB)—Therefore humble yourselves under the mighty hand of God, that He may exalt you at the proper time, casting all your anxiety on Him because He cares for you.

Proverbs 3:6 (NASB)—In all your ways acknowledge Him, and He will make your paths straight.

->> Rejection <<-

1 Samuel 12:22 (NASB)—For the Lord will not abandon His people on account of His great name, because the Lord has been pleased to make you a people for Himself.

Psalm 27:10 (NASB)—For my father and mother have forsaken me, but the Lord will take me up.

Matthew 5:11–12 (NASB)—"Blessed are you when people insult you and persecute you, and falsely say all kinds of evil against you because of Me. Rejoice and be glad, for your reward in heaven is great; for in the same way they persecuted the prophets who were before you."

John 1:10–11 (NASB)—He was in the world, and the world was made through Him, and the world did not know Him.

He came to His own, and those who were His own did not receive Him.

Luke 10:16 (NASB)—"The one who listens to you listens to Me, and the one who rejects you rejects Me; and he who rejects Me rejects the One who sent Me."

Psalm 37:23–24 (NASB)—The steps of a man are established by the Lord, and He delights in his way. When he falls, he will not be hurled headlong, because the Lord is the One who holds his hand.

Romans 5:3–4 (NASB)—And not only this, but we also exult in our tribulations, knowing that tribulation brings about perseverance; and perseverance, proven character; and proven character, hope.

->> Tired <<-

Jeremiah 31:25 (NASB)—For I satisfy the weary ones and refresh everyone who languishes.

Isaiah 40:29 (NASB)—He gives strength to the weary, and to him who lacks might He increases power.

Romans 8:26–28 (NASB)—In the same way the Spirit also helps our weakness; for we do not know how to pray as we should, but the Spirit Himself intercedes for us with groanings too deep for words; and He who searches the hearts knows what the mind of the Spirit is, because He intercedes for the saints according to the will of God. And we know that

God causes all things to work together for good to those who love God, to those who are called according to His purpose.

Colossians 1:29 (NASB)—For this purpose also I labor, striving according to His power, which mightily works within me.

Psalm 73:26 (NASB)—My flesh and my heart may fail, but God is the strength of my heart and my portion forever.

Matthew 11:28–29 (NASB)—"Come to Me, all who are weary and heavy-laden, and I will give you rest. Take My yoke upon you and learn from Me, for I am gentle and humble in heart, and you will find rest for your souls.

Hebrews 4:16 (NASB)—Therefore let us draw near with confidence to the throne of grace, so that we may receive mercy and find grace to help in time of need.

Psalm 119:114 (NASB)—You are my hiding place and my shield; I wait for Your word.

Psalm 18:31–32 (NASB)—For who is God, but the Lord? And who is a rock, except our God, the God who girds me with strength and makes my way blameless?

Psalm 62:5 (NASB)—My soul, wait in silence for God only, for my hope is from Him.

Proverbs 3:24 (NASB)—When you lie down, you will not be afraid; when you lie down, your sleep will be sweet.

Exodus 33:14 (NASB)—And He said, "My presence shall go with you, and I will give you rest."

->> Loneliness <<-

Deuteronomy 31:6 (NASB)—Be strong and courageous, do not be afraid or tremble at them, for the Lord your God is the one who goes with you. He will not fail your or forsake you.

Romans 8:31–37 (NASB)—What then shall we say to these things? If God is for us, who is against us? He who did not spare His own Son, but delivered Him over for us all, how will He not also with Him freely give us all things? Who will bring a charge against God's elect? God is the one who justifies; who is the one who condemns: Christ Jesus is He who died, yes, rather who was raised, who is at the right hand of God, who also intercedes for us. Who will separate us from the love of Christ? Will tribulation, or distress, or persecution, or famine, or nakedness, or peril, or sword? Just as it was written, "For the sake we are being put to death all day long; we were considered as sheep to be slaughtered." But in all these things we overwhelmingly conquer through Him who loved us.

Psalm 25:16 (NASB)—Turn to me and be gracious to me, for I am lonely and afflicted.

Matthew 28:20 (NASB)—"Teaching them to observe all that I commanded you; and lo, I am with you always, even to the end of the age."

Psalm 68:5–6 (NASB)—A father of the fatherless and a judge for the widows, is God in His holy habitation. God makes a home for the lonely; He leads out the prisoners into prosperity, only the rebellious dwell in a parched land.

Proverbs 18:24 (NASB)—A man of too many friends comes to ruin, but there is a friend who sticks closer than a brother.

Isaiah 41:10 (NASB)—'Do not fear, for I am with you; do not anxiously look about you, for I am your God. I will strengthen you, surely I will help you, surely I will uphold you with My righteous right hand.'

1 Peter 5:7 (NASB)—Casting all your anxiety on Him, because He cares for you.

->> Shame <<-

Philippians 3:13 (NASB)—"Brethren, I do not regard myself as having laid hold of it yet; but one thing I do: forgetting what lies behind and reaching forward to what lies ahead."

1 John 1:9 (NASB)—"If we confess our sins, He is faithful and righteous to forgive us our sins and to cleanse us from all unrighteousness."

Psalm 34:4–5 (NASB)—"I sought the Lord, and He answered me, and delivered me from all my fears. They looked to Him and were radiant, and their faces will never be ashamed.

2 Corinthians 7:10 (NASB)—"For the sorrow that is according to the will of God produces a repentance without regret, leading to salvation, but the sorrow of the world produces death.

1 John 2:1 (NASB)—My little children, I am writing these things to you so that you may not sin. And if anyone sins, we have an Advocate with the Father, Jesus Christ the righteous;

Revelation 21:4 (NASB)—And He will wipe away every tear from their eyes; and there will no longer be any death; there will no longer be any mourning, or crying, or pain; the first things have passed away.

Acts 8:22 (NASB)—Therefore repent of this wickedness of yours, and pray the Lord that, if possible, the intention of your heart may be forgiven you.

Micah 7:19 (NASB)—I will bear the indignation of the Lord because I have sinned against Him, until He pleads my case and executes justice for me. He will bring me out to the light, and I will see His righteousness.

Romans 10:13 (NASB)—For "whoever will call on the name of the Lord will be saved."

Isaiah 54:4 (NASB)—"Fear not, for you will not be put to shame; and do not feel humiliated, for you will not b dis-graced; but you will forget the shame of your youth, and the reproach of your widowhood you will remember no more.

Acts 3:19 (NASB)—Therefore repent and return, so that your sins may be wiped away, in order that times of refreshing may come from the presence of the Lord.

Psalm 40:11 (NASB)—You, O Lord, will not withhold Your compassion from me; Your lovingkindness and Your truth will continually preserve me.

Johns 3:17 (NASB)—"For God did not send the son into the world to judge the world, but that the world might be saved through Him."

1 Corinthians 6:18 (NASB)—Flee immorality. Every other sin that a man commits is outside the body, but the immoral man sins against his own body.

Psalm 103:8–12 (NASB)—The Lord is compassionate and gracious, slow to anger and abounding in loving kindness. He will not always strive with us, nor will He keep His anger forever. He has not dealt with us according to our sins, nor rewarded us according to our iniquities. For as high as the heavens are above the earth, so great is His loving kindness toward those who fear Him. As far as the east is from the west, so far has He removed our transgressions from us.

Hebrews 10:15–18 (NASB)—And the Holy Spirit also testifies to us; for after saying, "This is the covenant that I will make with them after those days, says the Lord: I will put my laws upon their heart, and on their mind, I will write them," He then says, "And their sins and their lawless deeds I will remember no more." Now where there is forgiveness of these things, there is no longer any offering for sin.

1 John 2:2 (NASB)—And He Himself is the propitiation of our sins; and not for ours only, but also for those of the whole world.

Romans 10:9 (NASB)—That if you confess with your mouth Jesus as Lord and believe in your heart that God raised Him from the dead, you will be saved.

John 3:18 (NASB)—"He who believes in Him is not judged; he who does not believe has been judged already, because he has not believed in the name of the only begotten Son of God."

1 Thessalonians 4:3–5 (NASB)—For this is the will of God, your sanctification; that is, that you abstain from sexual immorality; that each of you know how to possess his own vessel in sanctification and honor, not in lustful passion, like the Gentiles who do not know God.

Isaiah 50:7 (NASB)—For the Lord God helps me, therefore, I am not disgraced; therefore, I have set my face like flint, and I know that I will not be ashamed.

Psalm 22:5 (NASB)—To Your they cried out and were delivered; in You they trusted and were not disappointed.

James 5:16 (NASB)—Therefore, confess your sins to one another, and pray for one another so that you may be healed. The effective prayer of a righteous man can accomplish much.

Hebrews 12:2 (NASB)—Fixing our eyes on Jesus, the author and perfecter of faith, who for the joy set before Him endured the cross, despising the shame, and has sat down at the right hand of the throne of God.

Romans 1:16 (NASB)—For I am not ashamed of the gospel, for it is the power of God for salvation to everyone who believes, to the Jew first and also to the Greek.

Isaiah 61:7 (NASB)—Instead of your shame you will have a double portion, and instead of humiliation they will shout for joy over their portion. Therefore, they will possess a double portion in their land, everlasting joy will be theirs.

->> Confusion <<-

1 Corinthians 14:33 (NASB)—For God is not a God of confusion but of peace, as in all the churches of the saints.

1 Peter 5:8 (NASB)—Be of sober spirit, be on the alert. Your adversary, the devil, prowls around like a roaring lion, seeking someone to devour.

Proverbs 3:5 (NASB)—Trust in the Lord with all your heart and do not lean on your own understanding.

2 Corinthians 4:4 (NASB)—In whose case the god of this world has blinded the minds of the unbelieving so that they might not see the light of the gospel of the glory of Christ, who is the image of God.

Proverbs 2:1–8 (NASB)—My son, if you will receive my words and treasure my commandments within you, make your ear attentive to wisdom, incline your heart to understanding; for if you cry for discernment, lift your voice for understanding; if you seek her as silver and search for her as for hidden treasures; then you will discern the fear of the Lord and discover the knowledge of God. For the Lord gives wisdom; from His mouth come knowledge and understanding. He stores up sound wisdom for the upright; He is a shield to those who walk in integrity, guarding the paths of justice, and He preserve the way of His godly ones.

James 1:5–8 (NASB)—But if any of you lacks wisdom, let him ask of God, who gives to all generously and without reproach, and it will be given to him. But he must ask in faith without any doubting, for the one who doubts is like the surf of the sea, driven and tossed by the wind. For that man ought not to expect that he will receive anything from the Lord, being a double-minded man, unstable in all his ways.

Psalm 32:8–9 (NASB)—I will instruct you and teach you in the way which you should go; I will counsel you with My eye upon you. Do not be as the horse or as the mule which have no understanding, whose trappings include bit and bridle to hold them in check, otherwise they will not come near to you.

1 John 4:1 (NASB)—Beloved, do not believe every spirit, but test the spirits to see whether they are from God, because many false prophets have gone out into the world.

Jeremiah 17:9 (NASB)—"The heart is more deceitful than all else and is desperately sick; who can understand it?"

John 14:26 (NASB)—"But the Helper, the Holy Spirit, whom the Father will send in My name, He will teach you all things, and bring to your remembrance all that I said to you.

1 Corinthians 13:12 (NASB)—For now we see in a mirror dimly, but then face to face; now I know in part, but then I will know fully just as I also have been fully known.

Matthew 7:7 (NASB)—"Ask, and it will be given to you; seek, and you will find; knock, and it will be opened to you."